BUREAUCRACY AND INNOVATION

Volume 115, Sage Library of Social Research

RECENT VOLUMES IN
SAGE LIBRARY OF SOCIAL RESEARCH

BUREAUCRACY and INNOVATION

An Ethnography of Policy Change

Gerald M. Britan

Volume 115
SAGE LIBRARY OF
SOCIAL RESEARCH

 SAGE PUBLICATIONS   Beverly Hills   London

For information address:

SAGE Publications, Inc. 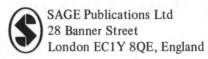 SAGE Publications Ltd
275 South Beverly Drive   28 Banner Street
Beverly Hills, California 90212   London EC1Y 8QE, England

Printed in the United States of America

Library of Congress Cataloging in Publication Data

Britan, Gerald M .
    Bureaucracy and innovation.

    (Sage library of social research ; v. 115)
    Bibliography: p.
    1. United States. Dept. of Commerce. Experimental
Technology Incentives Program.   2. Technological
innovations—United States.   3. Technology and state—
United States.   4. Bureaucracy.   I. Title.
HC110.T4B74   353.0082   80-26464

ISBN0-803901506-3
ISBN 0-8039-1507-1 (pbk.)

FIRST PRINTING

CONTENTS

Chapter 1

INTRODUCTION

In every society, under every political and economic system, public bureaucracies are becoming more powerful and pervasive. Government agencies influence what we eat, where we live, how we work—indeed, whether we are able to live and work at all. But few of us have had any long-term experience observing the intricacies of bureaucratic life. Even fewer have any idea how public agencies make the countless everyday decisions that affect all of us so profoundly.

From 1975 to 1977, I had the opportunity to examine the inner workings of one bureaucracy quite closely. A National Academy of Sciences Evaluation Panel asked me to assess a rather unusual federal program that developed cooperative policy experiments with a wide range of governmental agencies. Using techniques of firsthand fieldwork and participant observation, I conducted a detailed examination of the activities of the program and its agency partners. As a result, I was able to gain a unique perspective on everyday bureaucratic life and the ways in which policy changes were implemented.

This, then, is a book about the dynamics of the federal bureaucracy. While it focuses most specifically on the government's efforts to stimulate technological innovation, on a deeper level this is a book about innovation in the bureaucracy itself. It is especially concerned with the personal understandings and relationships through which policy change unfolds. But this is also a book about a particular governmental organization, an ethnographic study of the Experimental Technology Incentives Program of the Department of Commerce.

THE NATURE OF ETIP

The Experimental Technology Incentives Program (ETIP) was created by presidential mandate in 1972 to examine the relationship between public policy and innovation. When first conceived, ETIP was not expected to be particularly unusual. The President's Science and Technology message (Nixon, 1972) outlined a straightforward program aimed at improving the coordination and communication of research and development between government and industry. But in the early 1970s, American science and technology policy was in transition. More and more, policy makers recognized that sluggish industrial innovation was an important factor in our nation's lagging productivity and declining balance of international trade. At the same time, the government had failed in its earlier attempts to spur innovation by supporting the development of "big" technologies such as breeder reactors and supersonic transports. By the early 1970s, the search for a more effective means of stimulating innovation had begun. Since direct governmental intervention had proven too heavy-handed, attention focused on ways of improving the broader environment within which private-sector technological development occurred. ETIP quickly became part of this broader policy shift.

ETIP's founders believed that private industry was an efficient developer of new technology, but that a wide range of government policies adversely affected the social and economic environment within which industrial innovation occurred. By 1974, ETIP had decided to investigate a number of specific changes in government procurement, regulation, small business, subsidy, and research and development practices that could provide new incentives for, or remove existing barriers to, technological change. ETIP expected to be both a seeker of knowledge and an agent of change. The program intended to sponsor theoretical studies of policy alternatives, but its major focus would be on developing actual tests of potentially beneficial new policies with cooperating government agencies. These "experiments" would provide empirical data for policy recommendations, and simultaneously give agencies the experience needed to facilitate wider policy change. By working closely with agency partners, ETIP also hoped to increase the leverage and influence of its small professional staff.

When my research began in the spring of 1975, ETIP had been active for little more than a year, but was already implementing more than fifty projects. These ranged from simple contracted studies to complex multiagency experiments. Many of the projects focused on critically important policy arenas, such as regulatory reform, energy production, government efficiency, and environmental pollution. At the same time, it was already clear that ETIP was itself a far more significant experiment than any of its policy initiatives. The program represented a radical innovation in the process of policy change.

ETIP'S SIGNIFICANCE

During the 1970s, American innovation policy was dramatically altered. The importance of technological change to economic productivity and growth became widely recognized. Policy makers also gained a much stronger belief in industry's ability to innovate and a much clearer understanding of the limited role of government intervention. These changes occurred despite ETIP's contradictory and incomplete findings. Still, ETIP played an important part in the policy transition—as a cause of change, a result of change, and a basis for policy debate.

Yet ETIP's significance extended far beyond the program's effects on innovation policy. ETIP's policy experiments rarely focused directly on technological change, but were instead concerned with the effect of government activities on the broader social and economic environment within which industrial innovation took place. By modifying federal policies, ETIP hoped to shift private-sector economic incentives in desired ways.

As Robert Gilpen (1975) suggested in a report to the Joint Economic Committee of Congress, such policy "fine-tuning" has a wide potential applicability. At least in theory, the government can manipulate economic incentives to channel private-sector behavior toward the achievement of nearly any socially desired goal—from decreased environmental pollution to increased income equity or improved racial integration. After examining ETIP's activities, Gilpen recommended the establishment of a new government agency that would be solely concerned with tailoring the microeconomic impact of government policies. Although this kind of conscious manipulation has decidedly Orwellian overtones, ETIP's experience should at least give us a better idea of the extent too which such policy fine-tuning is realistically possible.

ETIP's policy change strategy was potentially even more important than its substantive interests. ETIP pioneered methods of policy experimentation that should be applicable in nearly any policy arena. In principle, such experimentation is simply the most "rational" means for testing the value of policy prescriptions. What's more, the idea of policy experimentation has gained increased support among evaluation and public administration professionals.

ETIP's experience provides us with practical knowledge about how policy experiments can be developed and implemented. At the same time, ETIP's experience also raises underlying questions about the whole policy change process. Experimentation may well be the most "rational" way to choose among policy alternatives, but bureaucracies are not necessarily "rational" creatures. Indeed, the limited nature of bureaucratic rationality is probably the most important single factor in policy change; it is also one of the central themes of this study.

THE GOALS OF THIS STUDY

According to classical organizational theory, bureaucracies are, first and foremost, "rational." From this perspective, ETIP might be considered the epitome of bureaucracy. Whereas most bureaucracies are satisfied to administer substantive policies, ETIP sought to enhance the "rationality" of the entire policy change process.

More recently theorists (e.g., Simon, 1974) have argued that the rationality of any formal organization is sharply bounded. A bureaucracy's informal structure, its social patterns, its place in a larger system, and its ties to a surrounding society and culture all impose constraints on bureaucratic action. Bureaucrats consider some alternatives rather than others, and their judgments are based on particular sets of values. Bureaucrats, moreover, are individuals first; what is best for the individual is not necessarily what is best for the bureaucracy. Personal understandings, values, and goals do affect behavior in the organizational setting. And the most basic goal of any bureaucrat or bureaucracy is not rational efficiency, but individual and organizational survival.

No matter how valid ETIP's policy change ideas may have seemed, they still had to be implemented. As a new and untested program, ETIP's first concern was ensuring its own existence. The program's options were severely limited by its relationships with other bureaucratic organizations, such as the National Bureau of Standards, the Department of Commerce, the National Academy of Sciences, Congress, and a larger community of interested scientists and policy makers. ETIP's staff had to interpret formal guidelines and develop the informal social relationships through which work was carried out. Because ETIP's business was policy experimentation, the program also had to encompass the interests and understandings of its agency partners.

In this study, the focus is on the practical implementation of ETIP's ideas. In Chapter 2, I consider the theoretical and methodological foundations for our organizational ethnography. Chapters 3, 4, and 5 then provide a detailed description of ETIP's background, development, and activities. Chapter 6 examines the personal understandings and social relationships that lie beneath the surface of everyday program activities. This provides the basis for Chapter 7's analysis of ETIP's progress, problems, and potential, and Chapter 8's assessment of ETIP's broader significance for understanding the policy change process.

Throughout this study, the goal is to understand not only what ETIP has accomplished, but also what it could not or would not accomplish, and why. Our emphasis is on how the informal social organization of the bureaucracy limited and directed ETIP's attempt at rational policy improvement. This is, in other words, a book about everyday life in the bureaucracy— about the ways in which alternatives are identified, decisions made, and actions taken. Although it is a firsthand account of a particular organization, it may help us understand the many other bureaucracies with which we must cope. Perhaps it may also help us develop future bureaucracies that better fulfill the needs of the people they serve.

Chapter 2

STUDYING THE DYNAMICS
OF BUREAUCRACY

Social scientists began studying bureaucracies nearly a century ago. Although most early research focused on the sources of bureaucratic efficiency, by the late 1930s the emphasis had shifted toward a broader appraisal of bureaucratic life. Much of this work was based on anthropological methods and models, and researchers conducted a number of long-term field studies. The goal was to gain a better understanding of the human dimension of bureaucracy, of the complex social systems through which the business of bureaucracy was carried out.

During the middle 1950s, however, such holistic case studies of formal organizations were largely abandoned. Generalizations were no longer grounded in firsthand observation, but were based instead on large-scale quantitative analyses of narrowly defined abstract variables. As a result,

the non-anthropological studies of leadership, organization, and administration provide formal deductive models, schemata, and tables of organization, generalizing observations, historical summaries and biographies, and even some laboratory experiments. They treat decisions as part of organizational behavior in a general and often static way. The natural place of decisions in the flow of organizational events in which they are only one kind of action is not precisely explored. Excellent as they are for their purpose, *these studies abstract the matter of decision processes out of context. The "process" is studied for itself, but not for its relations or functions within the overall context of organizational activity* [Arensberg, 1978: 71-72; emphasis added].

Indeed,

> The history of recent failures in social research points to the need
> for an anthropological orientation . . . [for] people with the ability
> to conceptualize human behavior into systems of interpersonal,
> intergroup, and interorganizational relations, to relate the structure
> and functioning of the community, and finally to integrate eco-
> nomic and technological with social data [Whyte, 1978: 131].

Today, after more than two decades of contradictory findings from large-scale statistical studies, a number of researchers
are again turning to firsthand ethnographies of bureaucratic life.
It is this kind of organizational ethnography that provides the
theoretical and methodological foundation for our analysis of
ETIP.

THE BACKGROUND FROM ORGANIZATIONAL THEORY[1]

When Max Weber first began writing about bureaucracy, the
realities of modern political and industrial administration were
just emerging. To Weber, bureaucracy represented a vast
improvement over the nepotistic and authoritarian character of
earlier patrimonial regimes. As logically designed social structures, bureaucracies more equitably met the organizational
needs of complex societies. Their cold, mechanical efficiency
was a necessary complement to machine-age technology and a
natural analog to the industrial work place (Weber, 1947).

Although Weber was concerned with the general relationship
between bureaucracy and society, his major contribution was in
analyzing how bureaucracies manage to operate so efficiently.
By now, the Weberian model is well known. Bureaucracies
achieve their success through well-defined formal structures.
Authority is administered through an explicit hierarchical
system. Work is divided into orderly spheres of competence and
responsibility. Workers interact through specified roles and
statuses based on consistent sets of abstract rules. Bureaucracies
are independent of personalities: Their members' individual
interests, goals, and relationships do not intrude into the work

environment. Being a bureaucrat is a career: Recruitment is based on universalistic criteria, and promotion occurs in a regularized manner.

In today's terminology, Weber's classical view of bureaucracy could be considered a "closed-system" model. Weber was interested, for the most part, in how a bureaucracy's internal structure influenced its output. He considered how bureaucracies could be most efficiently structured in relation to the technical logic of tasks, the delineation of hierarchical roles, the availability of professional expertise, and the use of proper incentives to motivate performance. Such a closed-system perspective is closely linked to the interests of efficient management and forms the basis for an extensive literature in "scientific" administration (e.g., Taylor, 1911; Gulick and Urwick, 1937; Moonay and Reiley, 1931; Brech, 1957; Allen, 1958). However, these approaches, like the Weberian model from which they are ultimately drawn, are concerned with bureaucracy only in a limited sense—in analyzing the effects of bureaucratic structure and its "rationality" on goal achievement.

Weber realized that his closed and determinative bureaucratic systems were ideal types which isolated the effects of a bureaucracy's internal rational structure. Weber chose to ignore nonrational and external elements which also affect a bureaucracy's operation. The personal characteristics of individual bureaucrats, for example, had no place in a model that divorced formal rules from private interests. Nor were patterns of interaction among the bureaucracy's members relevant, except insofar as they were part of the bureaucracy's formal operating scheme. The bureaucracy's environment—markets, clients, competitors, policy makers, and outside constituencies—were either ignored or treated as a depersonalized input that had no effect on the nature of the bureaucracy's operation. This focus on formal structure provided a simplified perspective that emphasized bureaucracy's rational efficiency and ignored various sources of irrationality and change.

After Weber's seminal work, a number of organizational theorists sought to develop a more realistic view of bureaucracy.

Although these students built on Weber's foundation, they were less interested in ideal models of bureaucratic rationality. Realizing that much more goes on within a bureaucracy than would be expected on the basis of formal rules alone, these researchers sought to understand the human dimension of bureaucratic life. They sought to identify the mechanisms which enabled self-interested actors to coordinate and cooperate toward the achievement of organizational goals. They sought to understand, in other words, how the formal rationality of bureaucracy was grounded in a more basic dynamic of social life.

This "neoclassical" view of bureaucracy (Scott, 1961; Thompson, 1967) focused on the study of "informal organization"—the everyday activities that occurred outside the formally defined bureaucratic roles, but which still had a crucial effect on a bureaucracy's functioning. Researchers delineated informal systems of authority, informal networks of communication, informal definitions of role and status, and informal patterns of organizational politics and individual goal-seeking. This informal organization was seen as a spontaneous and functional adaptation by human actors to the problems of bureaucratic life.

Anthropologists played a major role in developing this modern basis for organizational theory:

> While a beginning date for any field of study is necessarily arbitrary, it was the publication of the comprehensive report on the Western Electric Program (Roethlisberger and Dickson 1939) which set off in the 1940's a rapid development of courses and research projects focusing upon the human problems of industry . . . anthropologists were a major force in the early development of this field [Whyte, 1978: 130].

The list of early anthropological contributions to the study of organizational behavior is quite impressive. W. Lloyd Warner, for example, was a major participant in the Western Electric study (Roethlisberger and Dickson, 1939) and also conducted his own investigation of the dynamics of an industrial strike

(Warner and Low, 1947). In the 1940s, a number of important anthropological studies of informal industrial organization appeared (Arensberg, 1941; Chapple, 1941; Richardson, 1941, 1961; Davis et al., 1941; Mayo, 1940). By 1945, an anthropologist had published one of the first textbooks on organizational behavior (Gardner, 1945). In 1943, Warner established the Committee on Human Relations in Industry at the University of Chicago; by 1946, Warner and Gardner formed Social Research, Inc., an anthropologically oriented management consulting firm that exists to this day.

From an anthropological viewpoint, formal organizations were seen as complicated and living social systems. In reaction to earlier "scientific management" writings (Taylor, 1911), anthropologists emphasized the informal social groupings that were often at odds with an organization's formally defined rules. This informal organization defined "subcultural groups" whose members were strongly influenced by group norms, sentiments, and status-seeking. Anthropologists realized that formal organizations were far more complicated than their structural blueprints, and

> anthropology's methods of natural history observation, inductive generalization from participant observation, and open-ended interviews, and its use of sociometric measures of interactions among live human beings in real events, lately expanded into network and event analysis, made new and telling contributions [Arensberg, 1978: 51].

This anthropological focus on firsthand observation of social and cultural processes had a continuing influence on organizational theory, and a number of classic studies by nonanthropologists took a decidedly anthropological bent (e.g., Blau, 1954, Selznick, 1949, Gouldner, 1954, Whyte, 1955, Lawler, 1973). But the promise of the neoclassical approach was never fully realized. Instead of focusing on regularities in informal organization, ethnographic case studies soon devolved into ideosyncratic descriptions of worker psychology. Informal organization began to be viewed as simply an irrational, but controllable, input within an otherwise rational bureaucratic system.

By the mid-1950s, a new perspective for organizational research was emerging.

The "comparative structure" approach (e.g., Thompson, 1961; Pugh et al. 1963; Hall et al., 1967; Pugh et al., 1968; Blau and Schoenherr, 1971) dominated organizational theory for more than twenty years. It recognized that worker psychology, behavior, and culture varied, but considered them irrelevant epiphenomena. The closed-system model of the structuralists focused instead on what were considered to be deeply rooted differences in bureaucratic form. But unlike Weber, the comparative structuralists were uninterested in purely theoretical musings. They were, above all else, inductive empiricists, who collected enormous quantities of organizational data and analyzed them through the most sophisticated statistical techniques. Rather than pursuing detailed case studies of organizational dynamics in particular settings, the structuralists analyzed formal organizational differences in many settings. Over time, they conducted larger and larger studies relating such factors as innovativeness, leadership style, and efficiency to "structural" variables such as type of technology, degree of hierarchy, or scope of administrative span. Organizations were seen as Durkheimian social aggregates, independent of individual will and variation.

Eventually, the inadequacies of this approach became apparent. On the one hand, its survey methodology implied that

> researchers must content themselves with items of information that can be readily picked up and that are reasonably objective in character. Thus, while we may be encouraged to find correlations among a number of structural variables, generally correlations are at such a low level that . . . they provide little guidance to the person of action [Whyte, 1978: 134].

In other words, the methodology of large-scale comparative studies itself limited the range of variables that could be considered. Also, it became apparent, at least to some theorists, that those variables most amenable to survey analysis were not necessarily the most relevant for understanding organizational dynamics and differences.

Certainly, this was at least part of the reason that structuralist studies generally yielded significant unexplained variance and contradictory findings (Downs and Mohr, 1976). But even more important was the fact that the comparative structural approach ignored both the nonrational aspects of information organization and the adaptive relationship between a bureaucracy and its environment. Static correlations could only describe an unchanging present. The comparative structuralists produced some useful insights, but cumulative theory-building progressed slowly, if at all. Perhaps the primary reason, and what is the fundamental finding of this research, is that organizational dynamics is a complex, highly context-specific, multidimensional process.

By the early 1970s a new, processually oriented, "open-systems" approach began to emerge. Organizations were no longer seen as mere amalgamations of formal rules, but as entities that were consciously adapting to their situations. The nature of this adaptation was affected by each organization's informal dynamics, as individuals and subgroups developed their own understandings of the organization and its environment in seeking to achieve their own goals. It had become clear that the functioning of a bureaucracy could not be derived from existing formal rules, but was a complex outcome of internal social process and external conditions beyond the organization's control.

The open-systems perspective transcended any simple analysis of rational organizational efficiency. It refocused attention on adaptive processes within organizations and among them. It rekindled interest in the variable nature of organizational rationality itself. As a result, much recent research has focused on relations of power, control, and competition as organizations and their members try to optimize access to important, yet limited, resources. "Neoinstitutional" approaches (McNeil, 1971; Perrow, 1972; Zald, 1970), for example, reflect the influence of earlier qualitative studies, concentrating on the internal dynamics as organizations adapt to their environments. This is complemented by the emerging "French school" (Tourane, 1971; Karpic, 1972), which focuses on relationships among distinct institutional domains: interrelationships among an organization's rational operations, its cultural institutions, and its wider socioeconomic context. Also important is a developing neo-Marxist perspective (Braverman, 1975; Goldman, 1973; Buraway, 1975), which analyzes the place of formal organizations within the broader structure of modern "class" society.

One aspect of the open-systems perspective has been a renewed interest in the dynamics of informal organization. Recognizing the complexity of organizational process, several researchers have abandoned large-scale surveys which make many assumptions about organizational similarities. In effect, these researchers have gone "back to the start" (Radnor et al., 1978: 4) by advocating case studies that can capture the contextual and processual character of organizational life. In so doing, researchers may temporarily diminish the generalizability of their findings in return for empirically realistic models that can better inform later inferential testing.

By the mid-1970s, a number of researchers were again applying anthropological methods in conducting contextual case studies of organizational life (e.g., Kanter, 1977; Hill, 1976; Pettigrew, 1973; Gamst, 1977; Radnor et al., 1978; Whyte, 1975; Britan, 1977, 1978a, 1978b, 1979a, 1979b; Schwartzman, 1980; Schwartzman et al., 1978; Browner and Chibnik, 1979; Britan and Chibnik, 1977; Britan and Cohen, 1980b). As one of the nonanthropologists among them noted,

> anthropologists have been one of the few groups of social scientists willing to spend extended periods of time in the field to test their hypotheses. . . . Latterly, anthropologists . . . have become interested in social process . . . the present research has been guided by a concern for the elaboration of social structure, of social process. An underlying theme is that theories of organizational decision-making, power, and conflict require a processual form. . . . A further reason for the choice of these [anthropological] methods is the flexibility they offer [Pettigrew 1973: 54-55].

But what, precisely, does such an organizational ethnography embody? How can an anthropological approach help us better understand the everyday realities of bureaucratic life?

THE NATURE OF ORGANIZATIONAL ETHNOGRAPHY

Anthropologists study bureaucracies much as they study any other cultural setting. The goal is a holistic view of an organization, its members, and its environmental context. The focus is on understanding the organization as it operates—as a social and cultural system that defines the rationality of bureaucratic life.

The ethnographic method encompasses a variety of procedures and perspectives that anthropologists have developed in studying foreign lifeways. The goal of ethnography is the kind of richly textured description that can only be gained through extended residence in the field. By living, working, and talking with people on a day-to-day basis, the anthropologist begins to understand a social system from the inside out. This insiders' view suggests what questions are worth asking and what data are worth collecting.

The ethnographic approach is also cross-cultural. It approaches social life with the assumption that each local setting is in some ways extraordinary or unique. For ethnography, all aspects of a social scene are potentially meaningful and fully understandable only in relation to their specific cultural background, which can differ in significant ways even within the same society or organization.

Ethnography seeks patterns in the seemingly random currents of everyday behavior. The hallmark of ethnographic research is the observation, recording, and analysis of behavior in context—a systematic description of social systems that looks for interrelationships among particular behaviors, customs, rituals, beliefs, and values in terms of broader patterns of cultural understanding, social structure, and environment. As George Foster (1969) noted, such an ethnographic approach is extremely useful precisely because it encompasses a wide range of social, cultural, economic, and psychological variables within a single conceptual frame. This, in turn, means that the ethnographic method often produces important unanticipated insights. Through an ethnographic approach, seemingly inexplicable social processes can be explained in terms of the subtly patterned cultural beliefs, decisions, and networks that lie beneath the surface.

Although most anthropologists have studied foreign lifeways, they have always used the ethnographic perspective to separate what is unique and what is generalizable in each situation. Now, anthropologists are increasingly turning to contemporary social settings. They are taking the ethnographic theory and methods developed to study "primitives" and are applying them to gain an in-depth understanding of our own society.

In recent years, a growing number of anthropologists have also applied ethnographic methods to the study of formal organizations. Indeed, a recent issue of *Anthropological Quarterly* (see Gamst, 1977) was devoted exclusively to the topic of industrial ethnography. But how does such organizational ethnography produce its inductive insights?

Perhaps the most important aspect of organizational ethnography is that it is based on firsthand experience. The ethnographer's extended stay in the field and intensive participant-observation helps in understanding the life of an organization as it appears to the "native." Ethnographers build on this personal experience through a variety of more specific data collection techniques: physical measurement, censuses, open-ended and structured interviews, ethnoscience elicitation, historical and documentary analysis, survey questionnaires, network modeling, proxemic analysis, and psychological testing. However, all of these must be grounded in the ethnographer's deeper understanding of appropriate questions and necessary data.

An ethnographic approach to organizational dynamics concentrates on the social and cultural framework within which everyday organizational decisions are made. It seeks to understand differences in bureaucratic behavior in relation to differences in the social and cultural context within which this behavior occurs. It avoids the rigidity of the kind of "normative" or "cognitive" rules that formal models of decision-making employ. It focuses, instead, on how bureaucratic actors more generally perceive and interpret their environments, "integrating the elements of choice we call norms and structure" (Cicourel, 1974: 34). Such decisions are not context-free; they depend on a person's "cultural baggage," and they are not reducible to simple principles.

An ethnographic approach is especially relevant to the diffuse decision-making situations (Connolly, 1977) that characterize everyday organizational life. Such an approach emphasizes the informal social and cultural system that lies behind bureaucratic behavior:

> Treating decisions in context, as they are made in the ongoing flow of human action and interaction making up the life of the group, company, or other institution, means that they must be viewed not merely as judgments of persons, however bold or skilled, but also as events which have a necessary fit, in time occurrence, within a matrix of other events. Looked at as an element of a pattern of action, even the most abstract model of decision-making takes on new dimensions. The model one must use is no longer limited to the decisions themselves or to data gathering, sifting, and testing processes which the decider himself goes through. Necessary as these processes are, decisions are also events in a field of interpersonal action within an ongoing organization [Arensberg, 1978: 73-74].

A full-blown ethnographic theory of formal organizations is neither available nor desirable at this time. More than anything else, ethnography represents an approach, a particular way of looking at social reality. Ethnographic methods provide a means of obtaining realistic understandings of particular organizational contexts, but the specific combination of field techniques used will vary from setting to setting. Certainly, my own ethnography of ETIP was carefully designed with the program's unique characteristics in mind. (For a more comprehensive appraisal of ethnographic methods, see Brim and Spain, 1974; Pelto, 1978; Spradley, 1979; Williams, 1967; Naroll and Cohen, 1970.)

CONDUCTING AN ETHNOGRAPHY OF ETIP

Soon after ETIP was established, an evaluation panel was formed at the National Academy of Sciences. This panel quickly realized that ETIP was a complicated program and that a great deal of information would be needed to understand it. The panel wanted to know what ETIP was actually doing and how this related to the program's formal plans. It wanted to know how successful ETIP had been at enlisting agency cooperation, the degree to which issues of technological change were being addressed, and the likelihood that improved policies would be identified. More generally, the panel wanted a clearer understanding of what the program could and could not do, of the limits of cooperative policy experiments, and of the transferability of ETIP's policy change strategy. By 1975, the panel had decided to hire an independent consultant to conduct a field case assessment of ETIP intervention experiments and to evaluate ETIP itself as an experiment in bureaucratic reform.

After meeting several times with the ETIP panel, I gathered a research team and began my study in June 1975. Other members of the team included Ronald Cohen (Northwestern University), Michael Chibnik (University of Iowa), Ronnie Britan (Illinois Center for Educational Improvement), Angelique Haugerud (Northwestern University), and a number of research assistants. The research was divided into three phases, each of which utilized multiple methods and data sources to investigate a series of who, what, where, when, how, and why questions about ETIP operations.

After developing a contextual framework on the basis of background documents, the first stage of research focused on ETIP's activities from the program's own perspective. This not only included an examination of the formal setting within which projects unfolded, but also of the informal understandings, behaviors, and goals underlying everyday program activities. ETIP's skills, capabilities, and priorities were studied both as they were formally expressed in interviews and program documents, and as they were actually used in choosing experimental topics, negotiating with agencies, and administering projects. Quantitative summaries of project characteristics were developed to provide a basis for qualitative interpretation.

Research proceeded in an iterative fashion: Answers to one set of questions defined the next group of questions to be asked. Interviews with current and former ETIP staff members were supplemented by talks with knowledgeable informants in and out of government, and by the analysis of a wide range of documentary materials, including background reports, activity summaries, project plans, work statements, proposals, budgets, miscellaneous memos, and correspondence. This data provided the basis for a comprehensive description of ETIP activities, their development, and their place within the larger bureaucracy.

ETIP could not, however, be understood solely on its own terms. The program worked by developing cooperative experiments with other government agencies whose goals and procedures were often very different from ETIP's. The second phase of research therefore examined ETIP-agency interactions through detailed case studies of eleven ongoing projects that covered the entire range of program activities. These case studies considered the development of agency relationships, the congruence of ETIP and agency goals, and the reactions of agencies to ETIP actions. They analyzed the process of project implementation and how various implementation problems affected ETIP's own understandings and purposes. Finally, the case studies indicated the kinds of policy change that ETIP was best able to implement and the kinds that produced the greatest difficulties.

The final phase of research was devoted to analysis and to the collection of additional information, as needed, to round out the data base. This included a quantitative survey of project characteristics and a detailed appraisal of program variables, as well as follow-up interviews with ETIP staff members and outside respondents. All of this material was then prepared in a final report that was submitted to the ETIP Evaluation Panel and the Assistant Secretary of Commerce.

This book is based, for the most part, on data collected while I was studying ETIP from 1975 through 1977. It differs substantially, however, from the report prepared for the ETIP Evaluation Panel. Whereas that report focused on ETIP's success in achieving its formally mandated goals, the present book is concerned with ETIP's larger significance for understanding the nature of program development, the process of policy change, the utility of policy experiments, and the importance of technological innovation. This book is concerned, in other words, with what ETIP can teach us about the broader dynamics of the federal bureaucracy.

NOTE

1. This section is based, in part, on ideas that were developed in Britan and Cohen, 1980a.

Chapter 3

ETIP'S EMERGENCE

THEORETICAL BACKGROUND

Americans have always been proud of our image as a nation of innovators, convinced that "Yankee ingenuity" has been the key to our country's economic success. Yet, despite this common faith in new tools and techniques, economists have only recently recognized the importance of technological change as a component in economic growth. This realization has come, moreover, at a time of growing concern that America's international lead in technological development is rapidly shrinking.

In the past, most economists saw natural endowments, capital investments, and the nature of the labor force as the major variables producing differences in national economic growth rates. In 1957, however, Robert Solow demonstrated that

> considerably more than half of the increase in American productivity had been due to scientific and engineering advances, to industrial improvements, and to know-how of management methods and education of labor [quoted in Gilpen, 1975: 1].

In other words, the "foremost input to economic growth is the advancement and utilization of knowledge" (Gilpen, 1975). Subsequent research has shown that most of the manufacturing exports from advanced economies like that of the United States are new products which other countries cannot yet produce

27

(Keesing, 1967; Vernon, 1966; Hufbauer, 1966). Technological innovation is thus a major determinant of international competitiveness and domestic economic growth. Indeed, studies have noted that organized research and development accounts for almost 40 percent of the annual increase in U.S. productivity, and that the importance of new technology to American economic success goes back at least a hundred years (Nelson, 1971).

If rapid technological development were continuing, these findings would arouse little interest, but by the 1960s analysts became increasingly concerned that America's lead in technological development was deteriorating and that its balance of international trade was beginning to suffer (Weidenbaum, 1965; Nelson et al., 1967; Mansfield, 1968). Although technological innovation is only one factor in economic growth, inadequate investment in civilian R&D was seen as a serious problem for which governmental solutions were needed.

By the mid-1960s, the government was already making a major investment in R&D, with more than one-half of total R&D funding coming from federal sources. But the rate of growth in federal R&D expenditures shrank from an annual inflation-adjusted rate of 13.9 percent between 1953 and 1961, to an annual increase of only about 3 percent during the decade of the 1960s. The vast bulk of federal R&D funding, moreover, was applied to the development of military rather than civilian products.

Most of the funds for civilian R&D have traditionally come from private companies seeking profits from new products under the protection of the patent system. In the late 1960s, however, direct federal involvement significantly increased. At that time, policy makers identified a number of seemingly feasible technological projects that private industry was not actively pursuing. The government reasoned that private investment must no longer be practical in these instances: Either the costs of technological development had risen too high, the risks had become too great, or the profits had grown too dispersed. Even though the new products produced would eventually be sold for commercial profit, the federal government sought congressional approval for massive programs to support the development of such high-technology products as supersonic transports, breeder reactors, and improved mass-transit systems.

Although such massive programs often prove to be inefficient, the government had already successfully implemented large-scale projects to develop new technology for defense and space agencies. In defense and space programs, however, the government had purchased new technology for its own use. Products did not have to be sold to consumers. Profits for military and space contractors were assured, so long as products met well-defined performance needs. The only uncertainties that companies faced were technological.

Most civilian-sector R&D not only involves technological uncertainty, but also commercial risk. Even if government aid facilitated the development of useful products, these products would still have to be sold at a profit. And, as the histories of high-technology products such as the Concorde supersonic transport aptly demonstrate, innovations that are well within our technological capabilities may still be commercial failures. By committing enormous amounts of funding to "big" technology projects, the government would, in essence, be making an advance assessment of commercial feasibility. Experience has shown that the government is a very poor judge of the issues involved.

Technological development by private industry is much more complex than the government realized. Basic research and new product design are only the first steps in innovation; products must still be manufactured and sold. R&D itself usually accounts for only a small portion of the cost of a new product's development. Many research efforts never culminate in marketable products at all. Dozens of studies may be conducted for each product that is eventually developed. In the same fashion, several different products will go through a development phase for each that is actually manufactured. Underlying the entire process is continuing uncertainty, which should diminish over time as a product is readied for sale. At each stage, decisions must be made, and since costs increase, remaining risks should decrease commensurately. American firms have historically been successful as innovators, in large part because they have proven to be good judges, as the innovation process proceeds, of a product's potential for commercial success.

Despite the high risks of any single product-development effort, private companies are often willing to spend enormous sums for basic and applied research, because the potential profits from successful products are exceedingly high. However, since the precise nature of useful technology is difficult to forecast, companies will usually support a number of independent research initiatives. However, as conceptualization proceeds to research, development, manufacture, and sale, technological uncertainties decrease and commercial risk becomes a much more important factor in decision-making. The available information and the parameters of choice are different at each stage.

By funding the entire development of specific high-technology products in advance, the government would be making a de facto decision about potential commercial success on the basis of limited information at a very early stage in the innovation process. At this point, most private firms, despite their greater experience, would still be exploring alternatives. It is no wonder that the government, with less experience and more haste, should make errors. Indeed, the government's initial judgment about the need for federal funding may itself have been mistaken. The lack of private research dollars may not have been the result of market imperfections, but of inadequate commercial potential that was already perceived by industry. In any case, neither the risk nor the magnitude of costs has deterred private investment when conditions warranted. Witness, for example, the billions spent on R&D by IBM.

As the problems with federal technology policy became apparent in the late 1960s and early 1970s, a sharp criticism ensued (see Eads and Nelson, 1971; Nelson, 1971; Gilpin, 1975; Kottenstette and Rusnak, 1973; Mansfield, 1968; Eads, 1974). Although an expansion of government support for basic and applied research was usually endorsed, funding for specific high-technology commercial products was questioned. Critics realized that coupling technological development and commercial success was at best difficult, and that the government, with little experience, was extremely inefficient. Decisions about product development should, it was argued, remain in the hands of private industry.

At the same time, policy analysts also realized that many government activities, including those not specifically concerned with technology, affected the environment in which innovation occurred. Innovation decisions were not only influenced by direct R&D support, but also by the government's patent, antitrust, taxation, procurement, regulatory, and subsidy policies. How, though, could relevant policies be modified so that technological change could be facilitated?

This question was the basis for the President's decision in 1972 to initiate two new programs aimed at determining

> effective ways of stimulating non-federal investment in research and development and of improving the application of research and development results [Nixon, 1972: 8].

The programs that were established under this mandate were the Experimental Research and Development Incentives Program (ERDIP) of the National Science Foundation and the Experimental Technology Incentives Program (ETIP) of the National Bureau of Standards. The President's concern, however, remained focused primarily on policies that directly affected technology:

> The experiments to be set up under this program are designed to test a variety of partnership arrangements among the various levels of government, private firms and universities. They would include the exploration of new arrangements for cost-sharing, patent licensing, and research support, as well as the testing of incentives for industrial research associations [Nixon, 1972: 8].

During the first months of its existence, ETIP tried to translate the President's statement into an operational program. The result was a progressive widening of program goals into an investigation of the effects of a wide range of governmental

policies that influence the social and economic environment for
civilian innovation.

EARLY STAGES OF PROGRAM DEVELOPMENT

Underlying the establishment of both ETIP and ERDIP was
the assumption that inadequate cooperation between public and
private institutions was inhibiting technological change. The
programs were intended to spur innovation by experimenting
with government policies that would enable universities, public
and private laboratories, businesses, and state and local governments to combine their unique R&D capabilities more effectively. Because of their different locations and backgrounds, the
NSF and NBS efforts were expected to have rather different
foci. ERDIP would place primary emphasis on university and
public laboratory clients, while ETIP would work with industrial firms and associations on more immediate applications of
potentially useful technologies. Both programs were conceived
in terms of a rather narrow range of government policies
directly concerned with technology transfer and government
support of R&D. Their experiments with cooperative funding
and research arrangements would seek to remove organizational
blockages from the R&D enterprise itself. Both programs were
envisioned primarily as project monitors that would define
project types, solicit proposals, and evaluate results.

ERDIP designed its program in these terms. Its "experiments" were intended to encourage interinstitutional cooperation and to eliminate the "weak or non-existent sector coupling" that limited nonfederal investment and participation in
R&D. ERDIP's program areas were defined in relation to the
particular kinds of organizational problems to be overcome.
"Cooperative Research Initiatives," for example, would "test
incentives that would encourage universities, industry and government laboratories to undertake joint research programs."
"Research and Development in the Service Sector" would investigate similar "blockages" in service technology. "Human
Resources for Technological Innovation" would be concerned

with the professionals themselves, promoting interorganizational communication by "seeking incentives that would encourage personnel development and exchange."

ERDIP designed its program in terms of loosely defined "problems" and policy "solutions." Specifics, it would seem, would come from outside proposals. The ERDIP staff would monitor this work and eventually evaluate it to form policy-relevant findings. However, no clear idea of the particular kinds of incentives and policy options to be explored was ever formulated. Even ERDIP's eventual matrix of 676 policy alternatives remained curiously nebulous. To be fair, it is not clear that more explicit definitions would have helped. "Barriers to inter-institutional cooperation" may simply have been a research topic of limited potential. In any case, ERDIP easily slid into a series of projects that proved of little use in the development of more effective federal technology policies.

At first ETIP, like ERDIP, intended to investigate

> by actual experience in cooperation with the private sector, the usefulness of a variety of incentives and mechanisms to stimulate the generation and application of private research and development [ETIP, 1972].

In ETIP's early view, too, inadequate interorganizational communication was a major barrier to technological development. The program hoped to develop experiments that would establish "a cooperative arrangement involving NBS and a combination of private sector or state and local government organizations" (ETIP, 1972). ETIP felt that a number of potentially beneficial technologies were ready for immediate development, which was "prevented by communication barriers that inhibit the necessary flow of information and funds." At this stage, the program's purpose was seen as helping to "deliver technology to the market . . . in situations where technology is blocked by interferences or barriers that require corrections which firms or industries cannot provide unaided" (NBS, 1972). The concern was not with the general environment for innovation, but with specific technologies and particular (primarily communications) blockages. The original ETIP guidelines recommended that cases be found where:

(a) technology is clearly underutilized or misallocated for the public good;
(b) the institutional structure mitigates against technological development or innovation; and
(c) government action is likely to improve the situation within reasonable time and cost restraints.

It was in this context that Harold Glazer, who was appointed ETIP's first acting director in May 1972, began to develop criteria for project selection. The program's first priority, he felt, should be to pursue new product development that would lead to general economic benefits such as an improved balance of trade, the development of new industries, increased productivity, and so on. He also thought that ETIP might place emphasis on particular product areas, such as cyrogenics or lasers, in which technological innovation seemed especially important. Glazer also thought that ETIP could work directly with business to encourage product development. Letters of inquiry were sent to a number of private firms seeking to identify technological problems that government intervention could help solve.

Glazer, however, was only ETIP's acting director, and he faced serious organizational problems. He lacked permission to spend project funds and found it difficult to develop an effective staff. A great deal of time was spent simply defining ETIP's purpose and the kind of program activities needed to fulfill it. Even more time was spent arguing ETIP's case to the Department of Commerce hierarchy. Although Glazer's view that ETIP should aid the development of specific technological products seems inappropriate in retrospect, the idea never really went far enough to be tested. By October of 1972, Glazer had been replaced by a new acting ETIP director, Carl Willenbrock.

After Willenbrock's appointment, ETIP continued, for a time, to pursue the goal of supporting the development of specific high-technology products. However, the industry reaction to ETIP's inquiries proved extremely disheartening. According to former staff members, most of the responses were simply useless. There was a flood of inquiries from "incompetents," but ETIP could not get legitimate industries interested. Industry did not want ETIP money; there were too many strings attached. One project, a private/public consortium for fabric flammability research, did develop at this time, and has remained the project that is closest to ETIP's original aim of "developing new research associations, working with small inventors, and implementing specific waivers of regulation."

The weak private-sector response to early ETIP initiatives and the unwillingness of the Department of Commerce to release funds without a more explicit definition of goals convinced Willenbrock that a change in direction was needed. ETIP's objectives were soon redefined in terms of a far broader range of federal policies and incentives that affected civilian-sector technological change.

Willenbrock realized that "the interrelation of government and private sector is complex and not enough is known to predict the effect on technological innovation of change in government policy." He argued (ETIP, 1973) that the selection of initial policy questions should be determined by

(1) areas in which there exists considerable experience;
(2) activities traditional to the Department of Commerce;
(3) possible new partnership arrangements between government and private sector; and
(4) experience of foreign governments.

Three policy areas were explicitly mentioned: federal procurement practices, federal regulation, and federal assistance to inventors and small R&D firms. "Experiments" would be developed in each policy area based on specific hypotheses aimed at discovering policy changes that could stimulate innovation and improve the productivity and international competitiveness of American industry.

Although Willenbrock's program plan was far more detailed than earlier efforts, it still failed to specify which policies would be tested, what agencies would be worked with, and what methodology would be adopted. To an extent, Willenbrock's efforts were limited by rapid staff turnover, and by a continuing lack of spendable funds. After funds were finally released in April 1973, two major studies were implemented to delineate issues, policies, and agency partners for initial experiments. One study was concerned with the relation between government procurement and innovation, the other with regulatory barriers to technological change; both formed an important basis for subsequent ETIP efforts. Logically, Willenbrock's next step would have been to refine general goals and priorities into plans for specific projects. By the summer of 1973, however, it had become clear that another new ETIP director would soon be appointed.

Jordan Lewis had already worked as a program consultant for several months when he became ETIP's director in September 1973. Under Lewis, a new ETIP staff was organized, cooperative ETIP-agency policy experiments were refined and formalized, and the first experimental projects were funded. Lewis translated Willenbrock's still somewhat vague ideas into specific program activities that would test the effects of a wide range of policy changes and their ability to

> provide new and improved incentives for innovation while allowing the private sector to decide how it would respond . . . by modifying policies and practices that are the natural domain of the federal government [ETIP, 1974].

Lewis kept Willenbrock's three policy areas (procurement, regulation, and small R&D firms) basically unaltered, and added a fourth focus concerned with government R&D policy itself.

At this point, ETIP began feeling intense pressure to justify its existence through action: to spend money, develop projects, and show results. Lewis began moving very rapidly to define hypotheses and locate government agencies with which cooperative experiments could be developed. While there was occasional resistance to ETIP's ideas, agency relationships developed even more smoothly than Lewis had anticipated. By late in the fall of 1973, the first project plans were being drafted, and by early 1974 the first experiments were in place.

Lewis both continued and modified ETIP's earlier approaches. The trend toward a broader definition of purpose and a focus on general innovation incentives intensified. The need to work cooperatively with relevant government agencies was stressed and appropriate methodologies considered. Most important, general conceptions were quickly translated into action. Still, one can see a continuous evolution in ETIP that culminated in an active program. It is this program, defined by the February 1974 Program Plan, which provides the baseline for our study.

Chapter 4

INITIATING THE PROGRAM

Many of the projects described in ETIP's 1974 Program Plan were already being implemented by the time the plan appeared. The Program Plan did not suggest specific guidelines for future ETIP action so much as it provided a theoretical analysis of projects already in place. As such, the Program Plan served to legitimize changes in direction that had occurred during the preceding two years.

According to the Program Plan, ETIP's interest focused on the effect of government policies on the social and economic environment within which industrial innovation occurred. ETIP contended that nearly everything the government did could affect technological development by altering the social and economic incentives for private-sector action. Thus, in addition to providing direct support for basic research and for R&D infrastructure, the government also influenced technological development indirectly. Federal patent policy, for example, had a major effect on technological decision-making; tax policy altered R&D investment incentives; antitrust laws established limits for cooperative research ventures; and so on.

Many such policies, however, have very general effects. They influence all industries equally and they involve issues of great political sensitivity. However, there are numerous government activities that affect innovation, but have less sensitive repercussions and more containable effects. ETIP decided to concentrate on those policy areas in which specific agency responsibility could be identified and in which straightforward policy changes seemed likely to provide isolable civilian-sector results.

The four areas selected for initial investigation were procurement, regulation, small business, and R&D policy. These choices
derived from ETIP's historical development and its location at
the National Bureau of Standards and the Department of Commerce. The 1974 Program Plan added specific hypotheses about
the effects of particular changes in government action.

At this point, ETIP's primary goal had become

> the development of a set of technological change policy recommen-
> dations and the body of knowledge necessary for their effective
> use . . . pragmatic and effective methodologies that the federal gov-
> ernment can use in stimulating the entire process of technological
> change . . . within the economy in general [ETIP, 1974: 2].

The pursuit of this goal was based on the assumption that
"better ways" of stimulating technological development were
available, since

> except for a few special areas, there is no evidence that the Federal
> Government had defined and tested the policies needed to facilitate
> technological change for the general social and economic welfare of
> the nation [ETIP, 1974: 2].

ETIP argued that while it is not usually necessary for the
government to intervene in a competitive economy, because

> markets, supplemented by the wide variety of government programs
> designed to make the overall economy and particular pieces of it work
> satisfactorily, generally provide the appropriate incentives for research
> and development activity and for technological change as a more or less
> automatic byproduct [ETIP, 1974: 3],

there are particular circumstances in which free market incentives produce inadequate levels of technological change.

The February Program Plan provides several examples of such
circumstances, which fall into three categories: purely economic
"market imperfections," differences in public and private
appraisals of innovation benefits, and market biases created by

particular government policies. Inadequate incentives for technological innovation might exist, for example, in a competitive market where individual firms could not themselves capture sufficient profits from a newly developed product. A monopoly that inhibited competition might, on the other hand, find technological change unnecessary for the maintenance of its profits. In other situations, market uncertainties that are created or exacerbated by vague government policies or by unstable regulations may lead to inadequate technological investment. Government practices can also increase the cost of technological change, for example, when regulations delay investment payoffs or ignore industry profit structures.

ETIP decided to study possible changes in government policies that could either remove existing barriers or provide positive incentives for innovation. To translate this general theoretical orientation into an operational program, however, ETIP needed to develop a clear-cut strategy of action. While abstract studies might be conducted that would suggest a number of potentially beneficial policy changes, the risk in adopting such changes would be enormous—the failure of a recommended policy change could have severe repercussions on America's economic performance. ETIP therefore decided to adopt an experimental and incremental approach. First testing the validity of policy change hypotheses on a small scale would allow knowledge and experience to be gained at little cost or risk before a new policy was more widely implemented.

Even so, ETIP felt that the validity of policy change hypotheses should be well established and that its tests should have a potential short-term utility. ETIP (1974: 7) decided to look first, therefore, "at those areas where theory indicates a high likelihood of impact on the level of investment in the total technological change process from conception to use." Furthermore, ETIP decided to focus on issues for which agency responsibility was clear and for which policy alteration was realistically possible.

Agencies were expected to be active collaborative partners in ETIP experiments. Agencies would commit their own resources, formally identify themselves with projects, and make a commitment to policy change. To summarize:

> ETIP projects will rest on existing supporting hypotheses . . . that have significant apparent validity. . . . Specific policies contained within the scope of agencies will be formulated consistent with those hypotheses. . . . Field experiments or data analysis projects will be undertaken to compare the predicted results with observed data. . . . ETIP must provide both for the development of new policy guidelines and for their adoption by those agencies that are to use them . . ., iterative processes . . . that should lead to a generalized body of knowledge that will form the basis for the development of other policy guidelines [ETIP, 1974: 1].

The February Program Plan provides a general theoretical framework and a few examples that could serve as the basis for an investigation of federal policies affecting technological change. It does not, however, provide clear-cut criteria for the selection of particular agencies and program areas, and provides only a few general guidelines for future action. To understand ETIP and its changes, we must go beyond the Program Plan's formal statements and consider the organizational structures through which ETIP's activities unfolded.

ETIP'S STRATEGY

The February 1974 Program Plan formalized ETIP's division into procurement, regulation, small business, and R&D policy areas. Each of these areas was given primary responsibility for the development of its own projects and for formulating experimental hypotheses and methodologies in collaboration with agency partners. In most cases, agencies were expected to take charge of day-to-day project management, while ETIP provided funding to cover "exceptional costs," intellectual guidance to ensure methodological rigor and policy relevance, and a final evaluation to assess a project's broader significance, as well as any need for follow-ups.

The 1974 Program Plan did not provide generally applicable project selection criteria, but did outline a number of potentially testable policy hypotheses. However, since these hypotheses were illustrated in relation to particular potential projects, their applicability in other settings varied greatly. Some projects, such as the development of technology competency criteria for Small Business Administration loans, involved hypotheses that were only relevant to a single case; other projects, such as the use of life cycle costing in government procurement, delineated hypotheses that have been the basis for numerous projects. The 1974 Program Plan was not so much a guide for future action as an attempt to clarify the basis for existing efforts; it was a working statement, not a final plan.

The Program Plan makes it clear, however, that ETIP intended to be an "innovator" in its search for innovation. ETIP wanted to stir normally stodgy agencies from their lethargy; yet it did not want to be an arrogant outsider, but a helpful partner with whom agencies could work. ETIP hoped to excite interest in "better ways" of facilitating technological change, and also, as a useful by-product, to help agencies improve their own efficiency. ETIP was willing to assume the blame for possible project failures, and to provide the funds that agencies needed to try new ideas. Working with ETIP was to be an essentially "no-risk" proposition for an agency partner.

Although ETIP saw itself primarily as an active mover that would test actual policy change, the Program Plan also envisioned a more analytical mode of operation. In this regard, a fifth program area, Advanced Planning and Research, was outlined; its purpose was to conduct

> analyses and exploratory studies to provide an improved basis for the selection of policy tools for future investigation, and to provide more effective direction and evaluation of the already selected policy areas [ETIP, 1974: 39].

This was intended to complement the broader effort to develop and assess policy alternatives.

Ideally, ETIP hoped to combine rigorous theoretical appraisals of technology policies with the practical ability to work with existing agencies to test these theories. It would develop cooperative experiments that would gain the knowledge needed to formulate effective new policies that could significantly stimulate technological development. Yet, while ETIP tried hard to realize these goals, actual program activities have differed in a number of significant ways from what was planned.

OVERALL PROGRAM IMPLEMENTATION

When Lewis became ETIP director late in the summer of 1973, the program faced enormous problems. Although ETIP was in its second year of existence, it had not yet developed an ongoing program. ETIP's bosses at the National Bureau of Standards and the Department of Commerce wanted to see results. Pressure for action was strong and progress had to be demonstrated. A workable program had to build on the basis of a few still nebulous ideas, a holdover staff, and the preliminary results of Willenbrock's research. In retrospect, the program seemed headed toward imminent demise. Yet, by the end of the fiscal year a new program plan had been written, a series of basic projects had been funded, and a variety of future experimental possibilities were being actively investigated. Still, it was precisely this success—the rapidity of program development—that created problems for the future.

Lewis' first task as ETIP director was to hire a new staff that was sensitive to technology issues, able to work cooperatively with agencies, and capable of assuming responsibility for a wide range of projects. During the fall of 1973, area chiefs and assistants were hired for all program elements. Most of these people were lawyers, businesspersons, and economists who had little experience in government, but shared an enthusiasm for policy experimentation and a concern for technological innovation. By winter, only one member of Willenbrock's staff remained, and he had adapted to new approaches while at the same time providing a needed expertise in the intricacies of bureaucratic administration.

By mid-fall of 1973, ETIP began approaching government agencies to discuss possibilities for developing cooperative projects. A variety of means for developing contacts with agency personnel were used—informal friendships, past work relationships, even impersonal phone calls to individuals listed in government directories. Program staff found themselves with little time to develop broad theoretical models or rigorous policy hypotheses; instead, they emphasized the role they could play in solving agency problems and removing administrative bottlenecks. ETIP presented itself as a program without vested interest that was capable of providing intellectual and financial resources that would enable agencies to better achieve their own goals. To an extent, this was simply a matter of "selling ETIP's money," and the search for "better ways of stimulating innovation" was downplayed. At ETIP staff meetings emphasis was placed on spending goals and the need to obligate funds; the first priorities were finding agency partners, identifying problems, and developing experiments. "Targets of opportunity" had to be identified and implemented if the program was to survive.

ETIP's early opportunism may well have been a necessary phase. The program's strategy, after all, required active, collaborative partners, and at the beginning an emphasis on developing healthy agency relationships was important. In any case, the program began moving ahead rapidly, if a bit unevenly.

Although the February Program Plan saw "experimentation" as ETIP's primary concern, projects actually represented a wide range of activities. Several of ETIP's early projects did incorporate policy change as part of their basic design. These experiments, however, were not necessarily equivalent or comparable. Some, such as the early procurement projects, applied a single policy change hypothesis to the purchase of a single product; other projects altered a range of procedures within a single agency; and still others were concerned with multiagency technological outputs. All of these projects involved at least some active intervention, but none was a rigorously controlled comparison.

Many projects, however, did not involve experimental policy changes at all. "Experiment design studies," for example, tried to develop plans for future experiments, and "general studies" conducted background research in areas of potential policy importance. During ETIP's first active year, plans were also formulated for future "evaluation" studies that would assess experimental results. Still other projects organized conferences, seminars, meetings, and colloquia to disseminate information about potential policy changes and about ETIP's own activities.

Although ETIP did not accomplish all its goals for fiscal 1974, the program did become an ongoing reality. Experiments and studies were implemented in all of ETIP's policy areas and a number of additional projects were under agency negotiation. Indeed, most of ETIP's later activities derive from ideas that were developed in the program's first active year.

By the end of its first active year, ETIP was still far less experimental than either its program plan or public relations handouts suggested. By June 30, 1974, 32 projects were being implemented and nearly an equal number were being developed. Of the 32 active projects, 14 (44 percent) were experiments, while 18 (56 percent) fell into other categories, including 5 experiment designs, 9 general studies, and 4 classified as "other" (symposia, meetings, and the like). The proportion of "studies" was high. Moreover, except for the initial set of procurement projects, which were based on one of Willenbrock's early studies, few of ETIP's experiment design studies ever resulted in experiments. In ETIP's view, outside contractors proved insufficiently sensitive to program and agency needs. General studies, which usually focused on economic or policy analysis, sometimes provided useful syntheses, but rarely led to experimental follow-ups either. The 32 projects initiated in fiscal 1974 included 16 procurement projects, 5 regulatory projects, 5 R&D projects, 5 small-business projects, and one advanced-planning and research project (see Table 1).

TABLE 1   New Projects in Fiscal 1974

Program Area	Experiment	Project Type Experiment Design	Study	Other	Row Total
Procurement	10 (63%) (71%)	3 (19%) (60%)	0	3 (19%) (75%)	16 (50%)
Regulation	2 (40%) (14%)	2 (40%) (40%)	1 (20%) (11%)	0	5 (16%)
Research and Development	1 (20%) (7%)	0	3 (60%) (33%)	1 (20%) (25%)	5 (16%)
Small Business	1 (20%)	0	4 (80%) (44%)	0	5 (16%)
Other	0	0	1 (100%) (11%)	0	1 (3%)
Column Total	14 (44%)	5 (16%)	9 (28%)	4 (13%)	32 (100%) (100%)

TABLE 2   New Projects in Fiscal 1975

Program Area	Experiment	Project Type Study	Evaluation	Other	Row Total
Procurement	3 (60%) (50%)	0	0	2 (40%) (67%)	5 (33%)
Regulation	2 (50%) (33%)	1 (25%) (50%)	1 (25%) (25%)	0	4 (28%)
Research and Development	1 (50%) (17%)	0	1 (25%) (25%)	0	2 (13%)
Small Business	0	1 (33%) (50%)	1 (33%) (25%)	1 (33%) (33%)	3 (20%)
Other	0	0	1 (100%) (25%)	0	1 (7%)
Column Total	6 (40%)	2 (13%)	4 (27%)	3 (20%)	15 (100%) (100%)

Although ETIP developed several new projects in fiscal 1975, progress was slower than anticipated. By June 1975, 15 new projects had been started. ETIP's efforts were also still less experimental than expected. Of the 15 projects, 6 (40 percent) were experiments, while 9 (60 percent) fell into other categories—2 general studies, 4 evaluations, and 3 "other" (see Table 2).

To an extent, ETIP's second-year slowdown was simply an artifact of earlier optimistic listings of developing projects, but the program was also discovering that implementing and managing experimental projects took a great deal of time. Such projects required much more than simple monitoring, and the workload of ETIP's six-person professional staff was quickly becoming filled. Even more important, however, the continuing search for program guidelines and project selection criteria culminated in differences of opinion and a major turnover in personnel.

At the start, ETIP chose projects by pursuing "targets of opportunity." These projects generally had at least some technological relevance, but emphasis was on solving agency-perceived problems. This enabled the program to develop a number of "successful" projects, but these projects often failed to test rigorous policy change hypotheses. Efforts frequently developed piecemeal, rather than as a coordinated investigation of "means of facilitating technological change." Although a number of individual projects have proved useful, their theoretical underpinnings were often weak and their design did not provide an adequate experimental basis for defining future policy priorities.

By the summer of 1974, several staff members felt that it was time to take a closer look at the nature and success of ongoing activities and to delineate future priorities that were more explicitly and rigorously focused on technological policy. A series of memos and papers were written in an attempt to better define ETIP's mission, program area boundaries, project rationales, technology hypotheses, and staff responsibilities. Other staff members, especially the program director, opposed this change and wanted to emphasize the practical issues of agency interest, project management, program development, and publicity.

Matters came to a head in the fall of 1974 when three senior staff members—the chief economist, the R&D chief, and the procurement chief—departed. Several months of staff friction had already slowed ETIP's progress, and now, in the middle of the year, new personnel had to be found. In the next few months a new procurement chief was added, as well as his assistant, two regulatory assistants, and a new economist. The chief economist and the R&D manager were never directly replaced. For several months, however, ETIP was busy simply enculturating new staff members and managing ongoing efforts.

The questions that had been raised were not, however, entirely forgotten, and in fiscal 1976 ETIP began taking a more introspective look at its priorities, while continuing program growth at a slower pace. A total of 18 new projects were added, but only two of these were experiments. ETIP also added four general studies, seven evaluations, and five projects that represented symposia, meetings, or administrative fund transfers (see Table 3). Of the 65 projects that were developed between 1974 and 1976, there were 22 experiments (34 percent) and 43 that fell in other categories (66 percent), including 5 experiment designs, 15 general studies, 11 evaluations, and 12 "others" (see Table 4).

Changing project activities were formalized by a program shift in which Small-Business, Research and Development, and Advanced Planning elements were deemphasized, and responsibility for their existing projects transferred to new program areas (see Table 5). The Economic Assistance Area was created to investigate federal subsidy policies and to provide economic analysis for other program areas. The Experimental Methods Area was formed to coordinate evaluation efforts, but it also assumed responsibility for refining experiment selection criteria, designing more evaluable projects, and developing clearer overall program guidelines.

TABLE 3   New Projects in Fiscal 1976

Program Area	Experiment	Project Type Study	Evaluation	Other	Row Total
Procurement	1 (11%) (50%)	3 (33%) (75%)	4 (44%) (57%)	1 (11%) (20%)	9 (50%)
Regulation	1 (50%) (50%)	0	0	1 (50%) (20%)	2 (11%)
Research and Development	0	0	2 (50%) (29%)	2 (50%) (40%)	4 (20%)
Small Business	0	0	1 (100%) (14%)	0	1 (6%)
Other	0	1 (50%) (25%)	0	1 (50%) (20%)	2 (11%)
Column Total	2 (11%)	4 (22%)	7 (39%)	5 (28%)	18 (100%) (100%)

NOTE: Experimental Methods projects are included in relevant substantive program areas.

TABLE 4   New Project Summary by Project Type

Project Type	Fiscal Year FY 1974	FY 1975	FY 1976	Row Total
Experiment	14 (64%) (44%)	6 (27%) (40%)	2 (9%) (11%)	22 (34%)
Experiment Design	5 (100%) (16%)	0	0	5 (8%)
Study	9 (60%) (28%)	2 (13%) (13%)	4 (27%) (20%)	15 (23%)
Evaluation	0	4 (36%) (27%)	7 (64%) (39%)	11 (17%)
Other	4 (33%) (13%)	3 (25%) (20%)	5 (42%) (28%)	12 (19%)
Column Total	32 (49%)	15 (23%)	18 (28%)	65 (100%) (100%)

TABLE 5   New Project Summary by Program Area

Program Area	FY 1974	Fiscal Year FY 1975	FY 1976	Row Total
Procurement	16 (53%) (50%)	5 (17%) (33%)	9 (30%) (50%)	30 (46%)
Regulation	5 (46%) (16%)	4 (36%) (27%)	2 (18%) (11%)	11 (17%)
Research and Development	5 (46%) (16%)	2 (18%) (13%)	4 (36%) (20%)	11 (17%)
Small Business	5 (56%) (16%)	3 (33%) (20%)	1 (11%) (6%)	9 (14%)
Other	1 (25%) (3%)	1 (25%) (7%)	2 (50%) (11%)	4 (6%)
Column Total	32 (49%)	15 (23%)	18 (28%)	65 (100%) (100%)

ETIP's shifting focus was also reflected in changing fiscal 1977 budget allocations, which applied nearly half of ETIP's funds to a few detailed evaluations. Over a million dollars were also allocated for a major regulatory project that the Experimental Methods Area had helped to design. The Economic Assistance Area also started a large-scale study of federal subsidy. The Procurement Area, on the other hand, directed most of its resources toward simply maintaining ongoing efforts. Other program areas became nearly defunct (see Tables 6 and 7).

During fiscal 1976, ETIP again experienced significant staff turnover. By spring, the regulatory chief, procurement chief, and two regulatory assistants had resigned. A new regulatory chief was soon hired, an experimental methods chief and three assistants were added, and the staff economist became head of the new economic assistance effort. By spring of 1977, the Economic Assistance and Regulatory Areas had each added a staff assistant.

It is clear that ETIP's priorities, goals, and activities altered significantly in the three years from 1974 to 1977. Before we attempt to analyze this shift, however, the following chapter provides a more detailed look at the activities and projects that developed within each of ETIP's program areas.

TABLE 6   Project Funding by Program Area
            (in thousands of dollars)

Program Area	1974	Fiscal Year 1975	1976	All Years
Procurement				
Total	1319	1091	185	2598
Mean	94	273	38	113
	(n-14)	(n=4)	(n=5)	(n=23)
Regulation				
Total	739	732	1195	2666
Mean	148	244	598	267
	(n=5)	(n=3)	(n=2)	(n=10)
Research and Development				
Total	1194	254	72	1520
Mean	299	127	18	152
	(n=4)	(n=2)	(n=4)	(n=10)
Small Business				
Total	1171	214	3	1388
Mean	293	71	3	174
	(n=4)	(n=3)	(n=1)	(n=8)
Economic Assistance				
Total	297	0	515	812
Mean	297	0	258	271
	(n=1)	(n=0)	(n=2)	(n=3)
Experimental Methods				
total	0	40	1818	1858
Mean	0	40	454	372
	(n=0)	(n=1)	(n=4)	(n=5)
All Projects				
Total	4720	2331	3791	10,842
Mean	169	179	211	184
	(n=28)	(n=13)	(n=18)	(n=59)

TABLE 7   Project Funding by Project Type

| Project Type | Fiscal Year | | | All Years |
	1974	1975	1976	
Experiment				
Total	1399	1375	1210	3984
Mean	117	275	605	209
	(n=12)	(n=5)	(n=2)	(n=19)
Experiment Design				
Total	492	0	0	492
Mean	98	0	0	98
	(n=5)	(n=0)	(n=0)	(n=5)
Study				
Total	2038	214	505	2757
Mean	291	107	126	212
	(n=7)	(n=2)	(n=4)	(n=13)
Evaluation				
Total	0	297	1840	2137
Mean	0	74	263	194
	(n=0)	(n=4)	(n=7)	(n=11)
Other				
Total	791	509	236	1536
Mean	198	170	47	128
	(n=4)	(n=3)	(n=5)	(n=14)
All Projects				
Total	4720	2395	3791	10,906
Mean	169	171	211	182
	(n=28)	(n=14)	(n=18)	(n=60)

Chapter 5

PROGRAM AREAS AND PROJECTS

In order to understand ETIP's evolution, we need to know much more about the substance of ETIP's activities. In this chapter we will consider each of ETIP's policy areas, describing both what was intended and what was accomplished, the characteristics of individual projects and the changing overall character of policy initiatives. This chapter provides, in other words, the basic descriptive data that our analysis of bureaucratic life will explain.

THE PROCUREMENT AREA

Right from the start, ETIP's Procurement Area had an extremely narrow focus. The Procurement Area began by developing a few specific policy change hypotheses and methodically applying them in a series of product procurements within a single branch of a single major agency. Next, the Procurement Area disseminated these new methods to a larger group of agency personnel for use in a wider range of product purchases. Finally, these same procurement techniques were introduced at another federal agency, and among state and local government groups. Yet, precisely because of the narrowness of its policy focus, the Procurement Area maintained its emphasis on technological change better than any other ETIP element.

By the end of fiscal 1976, the Procurement Area had developed 29 active and completed projects (see Table 8): 11 (38 percent) "experiments," 3 (10 percent) experiment designs, 3 (10 percent) general studies, 4 (14 percent) evaluations, and 8

(28 percent) "other" (colloquia, conferences, and fund transfers). All of the experiments involved straightforward changes in procurement contracting procedures, and all but one involved the use of performance specifications, usually a form of life cycle energy costing. Of the 11 experiments, 7 consisted of single-product procurements for the Federal Supply Service; the remainder were multiple procurements with FSS or other cooperating agencies.

The policy changes that the Procurement Area implemented did not reflect theoretical considerations so much as ETIP's historical development. Procurement policy was seen as a potentially potent stimulus for technological innovation nearly from the program's start. The government purchases goods in immense quantities, but rarely obtains technology equivalent to that available in the civilian marketplace. ETIP argued that large purchases of improved technology would not only provide the government with better products, but would also spur industrial innovation by significantly reducing market entry costs and lowering development risks.

Beginning with this basic concept, ETIP began a more detailed investigation of the relationship between government procurement and civilian-sector innovation. In 1973, Booz-Allen Associates was commissioned to conduct a study of procurement policy alternatives and, after Lewis became ETIP's director, procurement specialists were added to the program's staff. These efforts yielded a better understanding of the economic effects of government purchasing, as well as some specific hypotheses about the technological impact of policy changes.

Prior to ETIP's involvement, the government usually purchased the cheapest products that met minimal design standards. Not surprisingly, these products were also the simplest and most basic, incorporating technology that lagged significantly behind that available to private consumers. ETIP argued that if the government specified performance needs rather than design standards and purchased products with the lowest life cycle cost (initial price plus operating expenses), it would not only

TABLE 8 Active or Completed Projects in Fiscal 1976

Program Area	Project Type					
	Experiment	Experiment Design	Study	Evaluation	Other	Row Total
Procurement	11 (38%) (58%)	3 (10%) (60%)	3 (10%) (23%)	4 (14%) (36%)	8 (28%) (57%)	29 (47%)
Regulation	5 (46%) (26%)	2 (18%) (40%)	2 (18%) (15%)	1 (9%) (9%)	1 (9%) (7%)	11 (18%)
Research and Development	2 (20%) (11%)	0	2 (20%) (15%)	3 (30%) (27%)	3 (30%) (21%)	10 (16%)
Small Business	1 (13%) (5%)	0	5 (50%) (31%)	2 (25%) (18%)	1 (13%) (7%)	8 (13%)
Other	0	0	2 (50%) (15%)	1 (25%) (9%)	1 (25%) (7%)	3 (6%)
Column Total	19 (31%)	5 (8%)	13 (21%)	11 (18%)	14 (23%)	62 (100%) (100%)

NOTE: Experimental Methods evaluations are included in relevant substantive program areas. Three of the projects included in Tables 1-3 (see Chapter 4) had become inactive by the end of fiscal 1976, reducing the total number of projects from 65 to 62.

improve the quality of the goods purchased, but also, in the
long run, save money. At the same time, this policy would
encourage industrial innovation.

Manufacturers normally spend funds only for developing
products that they feel can be profitably sold. Even if product
improvements are technologically feasible, uncertainties about
marketability may make private investment unattractive. However, by making a commitment to purchase improved products,
the government would ensure an enlarged market that could
lower the risks of innovation to acceptable levels. Of course, the
eventual effect of this policy on civilian innovation would vary,
depending on the characteristics of the particular products and
industries in question.

By the end of 1973, ETIP again turned to Booz-Allen Associates for a second procurement study. The goal was to identify
appropriate agencies and products for experimentation, and to
assess the effect of various intervening variables (product, production, industry, and market characteristics). Booz-Allen's
final report described several possible experiments using performance specifications, life cycle costing, and value incentive
clauses in purchases of consumer appliances by the Federal
Supply Service (FSS), the Veterans Administration (VA), and
state and local governments—all projects that ETIP subse-
quently developed. Indeed, ETIP had already begun contacting
potential agency partners well before the Booz-Allen report was
completed. By the winter of 1974, ETIP decided to concentrate
its early procurement efforts on the Federal Supply Service.

FSS proved amenable to the idea of policy experimentation,
and was especially interested in the use of life cycle costing
(LCC). LCC, after all, had been used by private industry for a
number of years, and had first been considered for use in
federal procurement nearly a decade before. FSS had already
been criticized for past purchasing inefficiency, and was considering a variety of improved procurement techniques. A Value
Management Office had been established, but administrative
rules at FSS permitted variations from lowest initial price pur-

chasing only in special circumstances. The kind of experimental projects that ETIP proposed were precisely appropriate.

When the FSS was first contacted, ETIP was just becoming active. The Procurement Area's foremost concern was to establish a good working relationship and to maintain agency interest. Although "stimulating technological change" was supposed to be ETIP's mission, presentations to FSS emphasized the cost savings and improved efficiency that new purchasing practices would yield. Several projects were quickly developed that applied life cycle costing formulas to purchases of high-energy appliances.

By early 1974, ETIP had transferred funds to cover the extra contracting and testing expenses associated with five experimental purchases: lawn mowers, air conditioners, refrigerators, water heaters, and houssehold ranges. As the lead agency in these projects, FSS was responsible for managing contracting teams, for developing new performance-based LCC specifications, for advertising information to new bidders, and for testing products. ETIP was represented in all project decisions and monitored project results. No ETIP funds were applied to the cost of product purchases themselves.

The LCC formula developed by FSS with ETIP's help focused only on the energy cost and initial purchase price of products; maintenance costs and operating lives of different products were assumed to be equivalent. This kind of "energy costing" made it relatively easy to evaluate the differences between old and new contracting methods. From FSS's point of view, the ETIP experiments were virtually risk-free. If life cycle purchasing reduced costs, FSS could take the credit; if LCC techniques resulted in purchasing the same products obtained in the past, ETIP would assume any extra cost and any blame.

ETIP felt that a single-year procurement would provide insufficient time for manufacturers to respond with new products and would indicate a weak government commitment to new purchasing practices. The initial experiments therefore incorporated three successive annual purchasing cycles. While the first cycle of experimental procurements might purchase improved products that were already on the market, ETIP hoped that by the second or third cycle manufacturers would be developing entirely new products in response to the government initiative.

Despite some unexpected delays in writing LCC specifications and in testing appliances, four of the five initial product procurements were successfully implemented. In three of these cases, the government obtained more efficient products than previously purchased, as well as substantialcost savings over the appliances' lifetimes. The second cycle of purchases achieved similar savings in 1975, but the third cycle resulted in little further improvement. Still, from FSS's perspective, the use of LCC had improved the quality of products purchased, while reducing their overall cost. But the effects of these procurement experiments on private-sector technological innovation were far less clear.

ETIP's primary goal was to develop "better ways" of stimulating the entire process of civilian innovation. Although the economic theory underlying the use of government procurement to "pull" innovation into the marketplace was fairly clear, ETIP's choice of procurement projects rarely considered the effects of important intervening variables. Thus, projects that were individually well designed were not well integrated into a coherent investigation of the effects of government purchasing on technological change. Each project had the same general rationale: The use of performance specifications in government purchasing could stimulate private-sector technological development. But ETIP made little effort to rigorously assess theoretically expected product differences. Several crucial intervening variables could have been considered. The size of government purchases, for example, directly affects the extent to which commercial risk is reduced. The scale of industrial manufacture is a major determinant of the cost of innovation. Similarities between government purchases and civilian products, as well as the level of civilian demand for product improvements, have a critical effect on the private sector's willingness to innovate.

Interestingly enough, the Booz-Allen studies discussed several of these factors, but ETIP was too busy getting its procurement experiments going to worry about them. External pressures to quickly implement projects made agency rapport very important. ETIP developed a successful relationship with FSS, but one in which agency priorities came first. Early procurement projects were "targets of opportunity." They fulfilled FSS needs, but were less concerned with understanding the relationship between public procurement policy and private-sector technological change.

Yet even if scientific rigor were irrelevant, ETIP could still have chosen those projects that would have been most likely to stimulate innovation. ETIP might, for example, have emphasized products that involved large purchases, highly competitive industries, strong consumer demand, or technological "ripeness." Instead, several of ETIP's product procurements seemed particularly unsuitable for stimulating innovation. While more than 90 percent of the electric ranges sold in America are self-cleaning, those purchased by FSS with ETIP's help were not. ETIP saw the procurement of only 8,000 water heaters as a potent stimulus for technological development, although the water heater industry is dominated by a few large firms producing millions of units per year, with typical production runs in the 500,000-unit range.

Nearly all of ETIP's early procurement projects emphasized energy and cost efficiency, goals that were highly valued by FSS. But the kind of technological change in which ETIP was interested was not necessarily limited to these ends. ETIP's very first project, for example, aimed at procuring less noisy lawn mowers. FSS, however, was unwilling to pay for product improvements of this nature. Interest lagged, and although ETIP continued to search for a formula placing a monetary value on noise reduction, no purchase had been made by the end of 1976.

Over time, ETIP conducted an increasing number of procurement projects with the FSS, but later efforts still emphasized cost efficiency and ignored intervening variables. Several new project suggestions were developed in another Booz-Allen study (Project 40), including procurements of automobile tires (58), ADP ribbons (59), blood tubes (62), cleaning agents (71) and oscilloscopes (73). However, all of these projects stalled and none had resulted in product purchases by the end of 1976. By 1977, these efforts had all been incorporated into ETIP's larger attempt to develop a comprehensive experiment development capability within FSS itself.

ETIP's Project 42 sought to "design and implement a systematic procedure" for FSS to develop its own new procurement experiments. A related project, 63, developed and conducted courses in life cycle costing for FSS contracting officers all over the country. In conjunction with these efforts, an Experimental Technology Office was established at FSS in 1975 to manage ETIP-related projects, and to coordinate with other FSS programs.

Despite a great deal of "planning" and "development," only the four initial procurement projects had culminated in actual product purchases by 1977. Beyond this, FSS had added "value incentive classes" to all its larger procurement contracts; had considered new "systems purchasing," and "innovation purchasing" options; and had sponsored a series of conferences and meetings to publicize new procurement efforts. Given FSS's strong interest in procurement cost savings, however, it seemed likely that the "umbrella project" (42) would be successfully implemented. By 1977, the project's "suggestion," "procurement," and "implementation" subsystems were in place, and a first group of products was being considered for purchase. Still, the long-term effects of this project on FSS procedures remained unclear, and any significant impact on civilian innovation was far in the future.

While developing the FSS projects, ETIP was also implementing another Booz-Allen recommendation, the development of complementary experiments with the Veterans Administration. The procurement of medical supplies presented new experimental possibilities, since the VA, unlike FSS, was the actual user of the items it purchased. The quality of product performance was a crucial agency consideration, and improved technology had a potentially direct relationship with improved medical treatment. Although the VA was uninterested in technology policy as such, it was concerned with a range of performance factors that transcended energy or cost efficiency. Moreover, ETIP's initial contacts in 1973 indicated that the VA had a serious interest in testing the use of new procurement incentives.

Since ETIP's staff time was limited, a private contractor, Ross Hofmann Asociates, was hired to help design a series of "federal procurement experiments for improved health care delivery." The company was asked to identify VA needs and to help select products for possible procurement experiments. As part of the project, the VA was expected to establish an experimental procurement office within its Testing and Evaluation Division and to hire four staff members to manage ETIP-related activities.

After a long series of problems and delays, the contract with Ross Hofmann Associates was finally canceled. By the summer of 1976, the new VA technology office had hired only two staff members. Although product specifications and contracting procedures were being delineated, no experimental purchases had been consummated. By the summer of 1977, only one product (a "patient eating bowl") had been purchased, and procurements of "portable oxygen producers" and "syringe and needle destructors" were badly delayed. Other products were at early stages of consideration. Progress had been slow and the future of the entire ETIP-VA effort was in doubt. Little had yet been learned about the impact of VA purchasing on medical technology.

In addition to ETIP's activities at the federal level (which included a stalled project with the Public Building Service), the program also developed "experiments" (75 and 60) with state and local purchasing offices. ETIP's partners in these projects, the National Institute of Government Purchasing (NIGP) and the National Association of State Purchasing Officials (NASPO), did not purchase products directly, but served as clearinghouses for state and local purchasing agents throughout the country. ETIP felt that it could gain leverage by using NASPO and NIGP as centralized institutions to develop specifications, test products, and disseminate information.

Both NASPO and NIGP experienced organizational problems in gearing up for a comprehensive experimental procurement effort. Yet, even when reports were finally distributed to state and local purchasing offices, they were more often ignored than used. Although small purchases of window air conditioners, maintenance-free batteries, bulk refuse trucks, reflective material, cut paper, and school buses were made, ETIP began doubting NASPO and NIGP's ability to coordinate so political an arena as state and local procurement. Instead, ETIP began to work with other federal agencies that directly funded state and local purchases. By the spring of 1977, ETIP was investigating experimental procurements of police equipment with the LEAA, school buses with DOT, and energy-efficient fluorescent bulbs with the Department of Energy. Two projects were also developed with the Forest Service to purchase prototypes of more effective tool sheaths and headlamps. These contacts with mission-oriented agencies were at least partially the result of a July 1976 General Accounting Ofice report which lauded the cost savings of ETIP's LCC experiments with FSS and recommended the wider use of LCC (and performance specifications) by other federal agencies.

ETIP's Procurement Area developed good rapport with relevant government agencies and successfully implemented a number of projects. Indeed, procurement projects accounted for the bulk of ETIP's spending during the program's first active year. This success in implementing projects resulted in large part because procurement agencies saw ETIP-suggested changes as relevant to their own goals. But the congruence of ETIP and agency goals was far from complete. Technological innovation was not a major concern for most procurement agencies. ETIP could never hope to implement many potentially important procurement projects concerned with benefits other than simple cost savings. Instead, "targets of opportunity" were sought that fulfilled agency goals while enabling ETIP to spend its money in a reasonable fashion. This "opportunism" hindered any systematic effort to investigate intervening variables that influenced the impact of procurement policies on the civilian economy. By 1977, only a few "experimental" procurements had been completed and, aside from ETIP's theoretical studies, little had been learned about the effect of government procurement on technological innovation.

THE REGULATORY AREA

Nearly all of ETIP's regulatory projects were based on the belief that regulation could impose unnecessary barriers to technological change by increasing market uncertainties, raising product-development costs, and distorting "free market" investment allocations. However, the Regulatory Area found it difficult to translate this "theory'. into a set of specific, but broadly applicable, policy hypotheses. Although ETIP's regulatory projects had a coherent theoretical foundation, they lacked a precise focus for practical action.

Regulation is a complicated subject. Unlike government procurement, regulation is decentralized, with responsibility dispersed to numerous agencies that are concerned with particular products and services. Regulatory decisions, moreover, are often controversial, with a variety of interest groups having a stake in their outcome. As a result, ETIP's regulatory experiments were both more complex and more varied than its procurement initiatives.

By July 1976, there were still only 11 regulatory projects: 5 experiments, 2 experiment designs, 2 general studies, 1 evaluation, and 1 project classified as "other." Two additional experiments were just being started. Nearly all these projects placed more emphasis on economic analysis than on policy change. Such research may have enabled ETIP to refine its understanding of the relationship between regulation and innovation, but few experimental tests of new policies were implemented.

ETIP's regulatory projects reflected the program's understanding of the nature of regulation. ETIP differentiated among "economic" regulation, which established rates; "standards" regulation, which specified product and service quality; "certification" regulation, which licensed products for sale; and "envelope" regulation, which defined acceptable business practices. Although each type of regulation was seen to influence innovation in different ways, ETIP's regulatory typology never went further than a heuristic appraisal of examples. It failed to provide a basis for operational policy change hypotheses.

When the Regulatory Area began its activities, it faced very different problems than did the Procurement Area. Since regulation was not dominated by a single agency, policy change recommendations had to be developed for a wide range of settings. Many desirable policy changes, such as alterations in rates, were viewed as probably illegal, since they would alter rewards and penalties without due process of law. Over time, the Regulatory Area therefore shifted its emphasis toward less controversial experiments in regulatory administration. In most cases, however, regulatory agencies proved to have little interest in technological change, as such.

One of ETIP's first regulatory projects, the Refrigerated Rail Transport experiment (31), did not involve a regulatory agency at all, but the Federal Rail Administration, which spoke for the railroad industry. In the FRA's view, a "critical shortage" had been developing in the availability of rail transport for perishable produce. The FRA argued that railroads would not invest in new refrigerated equipment because the rates established for this service by the Interstate Commerce Commission (ICC) did not permit an adequate profit on their investment. From ETIP's perspective the problem was the "procedures" through which rail transport rates were established. If these procedures could be altered to yield more realistic profits, several new technologies applicable to refrigerated "reefer" cars were ready for development. Possibilities for a cooperative experiment were quickly explored.

ETIP hypothesized that ICC rate-setting procedures failed to consider reefer transport as a distinct focus of railroad profit. ETIP and the FRA therefore funded a project that would conduct a detailed analysis of the economics of fruit and vegetable production and transportation in order to "document" the need for rate changes and increases. The results of this study would be presented for consideration at ICC hearings. ETIP felt that higher rates would result, providing railroads with the profits needed for investment in new equipment and technology. To further stimulate innovation, part of the study specifically analyzed new technologies that were potentially applicable to reefer operations.

The FRA's view of the problem was remarkably simple: Inadequate profits led to underinvestment in "reefer" technology; including detailed economic analysis in rate-setting procedures would encourage innovation by allowing "adequate" returns. Unfortunately, the solution to the problem of lagging reefer investment was not so clear. The railroad industry's own doubts about the future of refrigerated rail transport caused FRA interest to lag and the project became seriously delayed. Although the envisioned economic study was finally completed in 1977, it was by then out of phase with ICC hearings and had little effect either on reefer rates or on railroad practices. In any case, as project implementation proceeded it became clear that the transport of perishable commodities was a competitive business and that railroads were losing ground to trucks and planes. Instead of boosting new investment, increased rates might well make reefer transport less competitive and less profitable. Moreover, even if rail profits did increase, there would be no guarantee that these profits would be reinvested in new equipment or new technology.

Like the reefer project, ETIP's experiment (76) in electrical utility regulation aimed at improving the information on which rates were based, but it also addressed a number of more general regulatory issues. Project 76 was based on the premise that operating electric utilities had become so complex that the information on which regulatory decisions were based was frequently out-of-date by the time decisions were made. ETIP therefore began developing a multifaceted plan with the Federal Power Commission (FPC) and with a number of state utility commissions for experimenting with the use of electronic data-processing equipment to improve the flow and quality of regulatory information. Changes in caseload management, analytical procedures, long-range planning and evaluation, and rate structures were envisioned. As in the reefer project, ETIP argued that rate-setting based on inadequate data unnecessarily biased "free market" investment priorities and inhibited technological change.

In ETIP's view, modern data-processing techniques could help reduce regulatory "lag" and provide a more accurate depiction of "economic reality," resulting in rates that would encourage increased investment in technological innovation. Unlike the reefer project, however, the electric utility experiment developed general procedures for improving information flow that could be applied to a wide range of regulatory settings. The project included detailed studies of past regulation decisions and also sought to help regulatory agencies improve their ability to process information for themselves. Project 76's relevance to technological change was potentially great, but because of the broad focus on "administrative efficiency," this relevance was also rather diffuse.

Electric utility commissions regulate monopolies. In establishing rates, they seek to ensure a fair rate of return to private investors while at the same time protecting the public interest. Inadequate data certainly can limit the accuracy of an agency's long-range planning and can result in rates that are unfair to at least some interested parties. Moreover, since the FPC and state utility commissions viewed increasing workloads and the growing complexity of data as pressing problems, ETIP's help was welcomed. ETIP was able to assume the cost of experimenting with new methods as well as any blame for possible failure. Because ETIP focused on issues that agency partners saw as important, it was able to develop good cooperative relationships. But cooperating agencies had little interest in "stimulating innovation." ETIP's project descriptions played down the implications of proposed policy changes for technological development. Instead, emphasis was on increased regulatory speed and effectiveness. The idea that this might somehow stimulate technological change often seemed an afterthought.

ETIP, of course, realized that more rapid and accurate economic regulation would not necessarily increase innovation. If innovation served to lower a firm's operating costs, the existence of regulatory lag might actually stimulate technological change by permitting unusually large short-term profits before rates could be readjusted. Thus, Project 76 was less relevant to understanding the effect of regulation on innovation than to finding ways of increasing regulatory efficiency itself.

In February 1974, a third regulatory project (47) was implemented to accelerate the "establishment of standards and their adoption . . . by the former Atomic Energy Comission." This project also focused on new regulatory procedures and on change in regulatory processes.

As ETIP noted,

> many regulatory agencies must develop and promulgate highly technical standards . . . based on the state of technology . . . which provide the direct interface between technology and regulation. One way . . . is by means of consensus or "voluntary" standards. These are developed outside the agency by a committee of people with practical familiarity . . . and, once developed, they are tendered to the agency for incorporation into its regulatory scheme [ETIP, 1975: A-34].

The nuclear power standards of the Nuclear Regulatory Commission (and the former Atomic Energy Commission) were usually developed, at least in part, through such consensus procedures. This consensus process was fairly lengthy. Participants devoted only a portion of their time to regulatory deliberations while maintaining regular occupations and work schedules. ETIP felt that a number of simple procedural changes could greatly speed the standard-setting process. Given the technological nature of the "products" being considered, this could directly accelerate innovation.

In cooperation with the Nuclear Regulatory Commission and the American National Standards Institute (ANSI), ETIP hired Battelle Northwest Laboratories to coordinate changes in the "voluntary" standard-setting procedures. Instead of having technical experts interact informally, ETIP paid for the services of a full-time committee chairperson, for technical editorial help, for technical secretarial assistance, and for a meeting of committee participants. As might be expected, this resulted in considerably more rapid formulation of recommendations; what had previously taken "several months, now occupied only a few weeks." ETIP expected that these new consensus standards would also be of higher quality than the old.

Despite the project's apparent initial success, ETIP had difficulty convincing NRC to implement the standards suggested. It was also far from clear whether the speed with which consensus standards were set was really a crucial factor in nuclear reactor development. In any case, after the near-disaster at Three Mile Island, the creation of such technical standards has become part of a much more complicated, and controversial, political process.

ETIP's Project 85, developed with the Occupational Safety and Health Administration (OSHA) in 1975, was also concerned with the information-processing capability of a regulatory agency. Like the electric utility project, it used "technology to increase the information and decrease the time for the regulatory process." In this case, however, the goal was not to obtain more "accurate" economic rates, but to reduce regulatory "uncertainty." ETIP hypothesized that clearer and more rapidly formulated safety and health standards would help to avoid long periods of industry uncertainty, reduce regulatory compliance costs, and facilitate private-sector investment decisions. ETIP hoped, in other words, to reduce the "unnecessary" impact of OSHA regulations on the civilian marketplace.

Increased regulatory efficiency was certainly an important goal, especially for an agency like OSHA that had been sharply criticized for earlier ineffectiveness, but such efficiency did not have any necessary link to technological change. Although improved safety and health regulation could certainly facilitate industry decision-making and increase economic productivity, this would have only the most general effect on innovation. In ETIP's own terms, the results were neither "containable" nor "specific." The goals of the Regulatory Area seem to have shifted: Removing "regulatory barriers" and "freeing the market" became manifest aims; technological innovation was only an occasional by-product. In any case, administrative problems at OSHA prevented the project from ever getting off the ground, and by 1977 the entire effort had been canceled.

The shifting of ETIP's regulatory goals can be seen even more clearly in Project 88 with the Food and Drug Administration (FDA). This project's initial focus on new drug certification seemed to provide a clear test of a straightforward hypothesis about public policy and innovation. Certification was a crucial step in the commercial development of new drugs. The project sought ways to safely speed up the certification process and thus to directly stimulate innovation.

For more than twelve months, ETIP and the FDA discussed drug certification problems and especially the possibility of using early and rapid field-testing to replace part of the time-consuming clinical testing procedure for new drugs. There seemed to be a shared interest in changes that could safely improve the FDA's efficiency and, at the same time, facilitate the introduction of new products. Some of the envisioned changes in certification practices might even have been applicable to other agencies and other kinds of products. As negotiations continued, however, the project's goals were substantially changed.

By the time the drug project was implemented, ETIP and the FDA had decided that instead of abbreviating the certification process, they would actually add new field-testing procedures. Although the experiment was well designed to assess the effectiveness of alternative field-testing arrangements, the addition of these new procedures would be more likely to inhibit innovation than to facilitate it. Again, agency concerns had received the greatest emphasis—in this case at a cost of more than a million ETIP dollars.

The reasons for ETIP's changing goals were clear. Although the FDA was concerned that delays in certification could hinder new drug development, the agency's major responsibility was to ensure the safety of the drugs it approved. Faced with growing criticism of certification procedures and with the possibility that extensive field-testing would soon be legislatively mandated, the FDA wanted to be prepared. Because of its desire to get a drug project going, ETIP was willing to help with funding and expertise.

Although ETIP's Project 48 "in the regulation of pesticides" was classified as an experiment, it was actually more of a policy study than a test of policy change. The project's goal was to

> provide enlightened information on what alternatives may exist to foster the development of effective pest control systems which conform to national standards and to spark discussion as to what should be done to stimulate innovation with respect to safe and effective pest control systems [ETIP, 1975: A-35].

However, in many ways this "study" had a more immediate bearing on technological development than did many of ETIP's regulatory "experiments."

ETIP's partner in the pesticide project was the Environmental Protection Agency (EPA). Although EPA's primary responsibility was to maintain a safe environment, the agency realized that its regulations sometimes imposed excessive certification costs on new products. ETIP theorized that the development of safe and effective pest control systems would be accelerated if regulatory barriers inhibiting investment could be lessened. Therefore, this project examined

> action the Federal Government, and in particular EPA, can take to reduce the high costs of complying with the regulations and determine what might be done to otherwise provide an incentive for the

discovery, development, and use of new pest controls. . . . Among the changes being examined are the certification of non-federal laboratories for product testing; increased codification of certification requirements; the use of a revolving fund . . . based on royalties; and the effect of insurance [ETIP 1975: A-35].

Research on this project proceeded smoothly, and a final report was eventually released. Unfortunately, the value of final recommendations was never tested, since no policy experiments were ever initiated.

In addition to these projects, ETIP initiated several other regulatory studies. Project 8, for example, "an analysis of the dynamics underlying regulatory changes having a significant effect on innovation," collected a series of case studies aimed at

a fuller understanding of the forces which have historically been responsible for prompting changes in regulations which have had a significant effect on technological innovation [ETIP, 1975].

Although potentially important relationships between regulation and technology were considered in this study, it was never linked to the development of new regulatory experiments. Other studies (44 and 45) that hired contractors explicitly to design regulatory experiments also failed to produce any tangible results.

While ETIP's Regulatory Area successfully implemented a number of projects that increased agency sensitivity to innovation, technology often seemed an afterthought. The primary focus of most of these projects was on issues of regulatory efficiency and administration that were most important to agencies themselves. From the start, ETIP's Regulatory Area faced strong pressure for immediate results and it was easier to develop new projects successfully when they focused on agency-perceived needs. Without more specific policy change hypotheses or a clearer definition of priorities, ETIP found it difficult to channel agency enthusiasm toward technologically relevant policy experiments.

THE SMALL BUSINESS AREA

One of ETIP's earliest concerns was that "the rate of invention in the U.S., as measured by patent applications, is nearly static, while that in other countries is rising rapidly" (ETIP 1974: 9). ETIP was particularly worried because it felt that inventors and small technology-based businesses have historically "been major sources of technological innovations . . . sustaining industrial productivity at high levels and [contributing] to a positive balance of U.S. trade" (ETIP 1974: 9). Recent studies have supported this view: More than half of the important innovations of the twentieth century have resulted from the efforts of individual inventors and small businesses.

Under the directorships of Glazer and Willenbrock, ETIP envisioned a number of projects that would encourage independent inventors. Under Lewis, this interest became a broader concern for improving the general environment within which small technologically based firms operate. In this context, ETIP argued that

> small technology-based businesses, which have been key contributors of important innovation, find it increasingly difficult to raise venture and equity capital. They also face regulatory compliance costs that are proportionately greater than for larger firms.
>
> ETIP's interests . . . therefore focus on:
>
> (1) reducing unnecessary barriers to the flow of capital in these firms,
> (2) facilitating compliance with government regulation of small firms required to invest in technological change [ETIP 1975: 5-6].

By July 1976, the Small Business Area had developed eight active projects of which only one (with the Connecticut Product Development Corporation) was an experiment. Four of the remaining projects were studies, two of which involved the Small Business Administration (a third SBA study was scrapped). In addition, two projects were "evaluations" and another was an SBA symposium. Most of these efforts were implemented during ETIP's first active year. The slow progress since that time was reflected in ETIP's decision in 1977 to deactivate the Small Business Area and to deemphasize future small-business projects. Even so, the Small Business Area spent nearly a million and a half ETIP dollars, and several individual projects cost more than $250,000.

ETIP's relationship with the SBA, its major partner in the Small Business Area, has generally been good. Although the SBA had little interest in technology as such, much of the agency's business involved technology issues. The SBA, for example, often received loan requests and contract bids from small technology-oriented firms which it felt unqualified to evaluate. ETIP and the SBA therefore implemented a joint project (27) to develop clearer procedures for assessing the potential of technology-based firms so that the SBA could provide more future support for inventors and small businesses.

Of course, the ultimate impact of this project rested on the validity of ETIP's assumption about the central role that small firms played in technological innovation. But the project's preliminary results also indicated that the development of rigorous technological risk guidelines was nearly impossible. ETIP therefore decided to abandon the project during the summer of 1976.

ETIP's second SBA study (Project 28) examined procedures that the SBA could use to help small firms comply with new regulations that required technological change. The project's focus was not on stimulating innovation so much as on helping any small firm utilize existing technology when complying with federal regulations. As a result, the study's final report had only limited relevance to ETIP's broader goals.

The final SBA study (46) investigated the development of technical competency evaluations, which could be used to determine whether "small-business set-asides" would permit sufficient competition for government contracts. This project was closely related to ETIP's earlier study of technological risk, but was more clearly linked to SBA's own goal of supporting small technology-based firms. It was also consistent with ETIP's implicit assumption that supporting technologically oriented small businesses would itself stimulate innovation. By 1977, Project 46 was still at an early stage of implementation and its potential could not be assessed.

Even if all three of these SBA projects were "successful," they would still be at odds with ETIP's strategy of incremental policy experiments. The point of such experimentation was to gain knowledge and practical experience while avoiding the risks of large-scale policy shifts. ETIP's SBA studies, however, focused on major policy options that might be incorporated into SBA practice without any preliminary testing. The studies, moreover, often seem designed simply to support the views that the SBA already held.

ETIP's work with the Connecticut Project Development Corporation (CPDC) took a rather different tack. In this project (32) ETIP did not alter existing agency policies, but instead helped develop an entirely new institution, a state public technology corporation. ETIP hoped to determine the effectiveness of such a corporation on the American scene and to learn whether similar efforts should be supported in other states.

CPDC was a bond-supported public corporation in the state of Connecticut that was modeled after the British National Research and Development Corporation. CPDC's goal was to promote the economic and social well-being of Connecticut by supporting the commercial development of inventions that could encourage growth in local industry and jobs. As ETIP noted,

> CPDC has been chartered by the state of Connecticut to provide funding for product development efforts within the state, in those cases where funds are not available from conventional (i.e., capital market and internal company) sources. Product developers, generally anticipated to be from smaller firms or independent inventors, would be expected to seek CPDC funds after having been rejected by conventional sources [ETIP 1974: 33].

The corporation intended to become self-sustaining through eventual paybacks of royalties from successful projects.

ETIP's involvement with CPDC began when the corporation became embroiled in a serious funding dispute. After the passage of CPDC's enabling legislation in the early 1970s, the $10 million in state bond funds that the corporation had anticipated became locked in a court battle over the constitutionality of their proposed use. After being contacted by CPDC in 1973, ETIP agreed to provide $300,000 to support the corporation's initial product development efforts while the court battle was being decided. In return, ETIP received access to data on all CPDC activities, including methods of product selection, funding criteria, product success, administrative problems, and so forth. Later, ETIP hired a contractor to conduct an "evaluation" of CPDC (Project 78) and hired CPDC's director to write a program case history (Project 89). As a result, the total cost of ETIP's CPDC involvement came to nearly half a million dollars. ETIP expected this investment to yield a better understanding of the potential of public technology corporations in the United States, as well as guidelines for their development and operation. The CPDC project was based on an implicit assumption that regular-venture capital markets had insufficient funds to support the development of many worthwhile innovations. However, ETIP also sponsored a separate major study of the venture capital markets themselves (Project 9). Some of this study's findings seem to contradict ETIP's earlier assumptions, which were the basis for the CPDC effort.

ETIP's venture capital study investigated market imperfections that could limit the availability of private development funds for deserving inventors and firms. Although the study concluded that the venture capital business was extremely complicated, it also found that it was remarkably efficient. The study concluded that American venture capitalists were usually accurate in their assessments of the potential of new technologies and that private development funds were readily available, given reasonable levels of risk.

Interestingly, some of the major criticisms of CPDC by venture capitalists focused on the corporation's inexperience in making decisions about commercial and technological risk.

Since inventors and developers of more desirable products could successfully obtain cheaper capital from private markets, critics argued that CPDC was left with only high-risk rejects to support. It might be noted that a similar criticism could also be aimed at the SBA's attempt to define technological risk criteria as a basis for government support.

The venture capital study remains hypothetical and was, in any case, concerned only with economic imperfections. A need for government action might still exist to compensate, for example, for the ups and downs of long-term economic cycles. But, at least according to ETIP's avowed strategy, major policy changes (such as those envisioned by the SBA) should not have been initiated on the basis of abstract studies with potentially unwarrented assumptions. Policy experimentation and incremental change was supposed to be a much more appropriate form of action.

Although ETIP's Small Business Area developed some potentially important studies and an interesting experiment, its place within ETIP remained somewhat anomalous. Unlike other policy areas, small-business projects rarely focused on incremental policy changes with existing agencies. Originally, the Small Business Area expected to work directly with inventors and small technology-based firms. After the fall of 1973, ETIP instead decided to work with cooperating agency partners. The Small Business Administration was a natural client, but one that had little direct interest in technology, inventors, or technology-based firms. SBA was concerned, however, that its work was hindered by its inexperience in technological assessment. ETIP's help was therefore perceived as a means by which SBA influence could be expanded to hitherto unreachable areas.

SBA was more interested in policy studies than in policy experiments. It was concerned with the effect of technology issues on its ability to support small business, not with the effect of small businesses on technological development. In consequence, ETIP/SBA projects often seem much more concerned with SBA administration than with civilian innovation. At best, ETIP's policy studies would eventually lead to SBA actions that might help small technology-based firms encourage long-term technological growth.

ETIP's original small-business aims were more directly realized through the Connecticut Product Development Corporation project. Even if CPDC ultimately failed, the project would still provide useful information about the value of such public technology corporations. The experiment would also add substantial real-world data to ETIP's venture capital study.

THE RESEARCH AND DEVELOPMENT AREA

ETIP's Research and Development Area focused more directly on innovation than on any other program element. Whereas other policy areas examined the indirect effects of government activities on technology, the Research and Development Area was concerned with the adequacy of government technology policy itself. Although the federal government provided substantial R&D support, ETIP argued that these funds were often used inefficiently. Despite successful defense and space programs, "relatively little effort [was] made to understand how federally funded civilian R&D [could] most effectively be conducted for 'improving the applications of research and development results' " (ETIP, 1974). This was caused by the fact that "agencies that sponsor applied civilian R&D typically give little thought to the use of their R&D results before and during the conduct of the R&D. As a consequence, the application of this R&D . . . is widely recognized as being very poor" (ETIP, 1974).

Five R&D projects, two experiments, two studies, and one project classified as "other" were implemented soon after ETIP became active in 1974. Later, three small-scale evaluations and two disseminations were funded for a total of ten R&D projects. Five more experiments and eight studies were planned, but died in the conceptual-development stage. By early 1975, the ETIP Evaluation Panel began raising serious questions about the adequacy of ETIP's understanding of the complex issues involved in R&D policy. As a result, ETIP decided to deemphasize the R&D Area. By 1977, new projects involving direct federal support for technological development were included in ETIP's Economic Assistance Area.

ETIP's description of possible R&D policy changes in the 1974 Program Plan often lacked specificity. When the Program Plan was written, potential agency partners were only just being contacted and project designs were still being formulated. As actual projects were developed, policy issues were clarified, but this moved the R&D program area in somewhat different directions than had been originally intended. Emphasis was placed on two general areas: the investigation of procedures for agency R&D planning and administration, and the development of new R&D policies, such as contractor cost-sharing, that were more sensitive to commercial markets and commercial development needs. As ETIP's August 1975 Progress Report noted,

> ETIP's interests with respect to civilian R&D focus on tentative policy recommendations such as:
>
> (1) Create formal R&D market planning functions in R&D agencies. . . .
> (2) Require substantial non-federal cost-sharing in development and demonstration projects.
> (3) View demonstration projects as field experiments that are experimenting with the field, and conduct them only when technological uncertainties have been reduced to low levels.
> (4) Obtain strong user involvement in the design of R&D programs [ETIP, 1975: 5].

These recommendations reflect a combination of the theoretical interests expressed in the 1974 Program Plan and the practical problems that emerged as projects were developed.

ETIP's first R&D project (7) supported a cooperative university, industry, and government study of fabric flammability. This project was initiated during the summer of 1973, and its planning predates Lewis's arrival as ETIP director. In 1972, Congress mandated funds for an expanded fire, textile, and fabric-flammability research program, and ETIP was selected to organize and monitor a cooperative research consortium. This reflected ETIP's original intention of focusing on patterns of institutional communications. Later, after ETIP's emphasis shifted, the fabric-flammability project remained the program's only attempt to develop new kinds of cooperative R&D arrangements.

The fabric-flammability project's underlying hypothesis was that the varying social, cultural, and intellectual perspectives of scientists working in different R&D institutions created barriers to communication and hindered technological development. The project, therefore, sought to help academic, business, and government researchers work together rather than at cross-purposes. The research consortium was intended to provide a setting where basic research, technological development, and commercial sales could be effectively coordinated.

ETIP began the project by asking prospective research consortia to formulate their own organizational schemes and submit them to ETIP for evaluation. In addition to the general focus on fabric flammability, criteria for proposal selection included "the social and economic rationale presented for the selection of the specific problem to be addressed by the contractor" (ETIP, 1975: 39) and an emphasis on "the proposer's plan to pursue early commercialization of the research results" (ETIP, 1975: 39). On the basis of the proposals, a consortium headed by Clemson University was chosen to conduct the work. Other consortium participants included the University of Maryland, the Polytechnic Institute of New York, Research Triangle Institute, the U.S. Department of Agriculture's New Orleans Laboratory, Hooker Chemical and Plastics Company, American Enka, Dow-Corning, and the United Merchants and Manufacturers.

The project's first step was for the consortium to conduct basic research into flame retardants for cotton-polyester blend fabrics. ETIP noted that very promising results were obtained in this phase:

It is now possible to preduct with a high degree of certainty, the types of chemical agents which could be effective in rendering

cotton and polyester fabrics flame retardant . . . to predict the effect
of given flame retardants on the flammability of both the individual
fibers and the blend . . . to determine the effect of various distribu-
tions of flame retardant chemicals. . . . This has major implications
for the optimization of flame retardant application technology
[ETIP, 1975].

After this preliminary research was completed, the consortium
began to investigate the effectiveness and commercial applicability of four specific flame-retardant methods.

ETIP was optimistic that better methods of retarding fabric
flammability were being developed, but was uncertain whether
the research consortium would speed the development of commercial products. Research consortia had been organized
before, and the project's lack of any experimental design meant
that it would be difficult to disentangle specific effects. ETIP,
in any case, followed its initial effort with additional projects
(125 and 126) aimed at disseminating the consortium's research
results.

ETIP's Project 67 was also oriented toward commerical development and technology transfer issues, but it was explicitly
focused on a particular technology—the construction of integrated utility systems at universities or médical centers. The
project's goal was to develop a new kind of demonstration
project that could facilitate the transfer of socially desirable
technological improvements. The specific changes that were
envisioned from more traditional demonstrations included the
use of contractor and user cost-sharing. These changes were
intended to ensure that contractors would not seek profit
merely by conducting R&D, but would also be committed to
later commercial sales; and to assure that users would see real
benefits, other than the availability of government funding, in
adopting new technology.

Integrated utility systems (IUS) were by-products of space
program research on self-contained environments. IUS combined five utility systems—water, heat, electricity, sewage, and
liquid waste—within a single unit, and by recycling energy and
materials achieved a significant overall energy and cost savings,
compared to conventional units. Before ETIP's involvement,

several government agencies, headed by NASA and HUD, had been investigating the applicability of Modular Integrated Utility Systems (MIUS) to commercial housing. By the early 1970s, most of the basic scientific and engineering questions had been successfully resolved.

In 1973 the Department of Health, Education and Welfare (HEW) joined the MIUS effort. HEW began considering the possibility of large-scale MIUS applications that would meet the needs of the health and educational facilities HEW served. The focal point for this effort was the Planning and Development Department of HEW's Office of Facilities Engineering and Property Management (OFEPM). OFEPM was convinced that IUS had a great potential for energy and cost savings in institutional settings, but it had no implementation funds of its own. OFEPM began seeking a sponsor for a demonstration project that would help apply IUS technology to commercial use. In the fall of 1973 discussions between ETIP and OFEPM began.

Right from the start of those negotiations, ETIP's interest was in something more than a traditional demonstration project. In ETIP's view, such demonstration projects often developed efficient hardware that was commercially impractical and thus untransferable to the private sector. ETIP believed that demonstration projects would be more effective if contractors and users shared in their cost. Eventually, a joint ETIP/OFEPM project was developed along these lines.

However, ETIP soon learned that architecture and engineering firms viewed such cost-sharing as unreasonable—a failure to pay for work done. As a result, the contractor cost-sharing provision of the project was quickly dropped. The project became a detailed feasibility design study entirely funded by ETIP. The architectural and engineering contractor first reviewed the general problems of applying IUS to institutional settings, and then developed a list of potential hosts. Two sites, the University of Florida and the University of Central Michigan, were selected from this list, and IUS installations were designed specifically for them. The institutions made nonbinding agreements that they would "try" to proceed with construction when the design was completed.

Project 67 took rather different course than was originally intended. Although two IUS installations were designed, the

contractor's willingness to pursue further commercial development remained uncertain. By 1977, neither IUS installation had
yet being built. In fact, both host institutions were seeking
outside financing for the construction through other sources of
government aid—hardly the sort of user involvement that ETIP
had sought. The project, for all practical purposes, had become
merely the first stage in an ordinary demonstration project,
albeit one in which funding would be coming from multiple
sources.

Still, several interesting issues were raised, since such detailed
feasibility studies represented potentially less expensive, and
little used, options to full-scale pilot tests. However, the IUS
project was not developed as a rigorous experiment and provided little new information about the appropriateness of such
alternative forms of technology transfer.

ETIP's final R&D experiment (13) was a cooperative effort
with the National Science Foundation to encourage university
scientists to seek commercial applications for their research
results. Planning for this project began in the fall of 1973, and
by spring of 1974 a contractor had been hired to develop a
"systematic 'awareness' program," to be implemented at
selected universities. This program was intended to increase
"the diffusion of university research output" by increasing rates
of patent applications by university scientists. The contractor,
Research Corporation of America, organized "awareness" teams
that met with scientists and engineers at the University of
Georgia, the University of Maryland, the University of Michigan, and Princeton University. Assessing the success of this
effort, ETIP noted that

> the number of invention disclosures that have resulted from the first
> and follow-up visits at Georgia has been at a continuing rate where
> monthly number of disclosures is exceeding the number disclosed
> annually prior to this project activity [ETIP, 1975: A-41].

The patent project fit closely into ETIP's earliest understanding of program goals. The project was directly concerned with
inventors and with improving communications between university researchers and industrial developers. The project implicitly

assumed that the failure of university researchers to patent their discoveries was itself an important barrier to commercial development. It also hypothesized that lagging patent applications resulted primarily from insufficient knowledge and experience with the patent system. In ETIP's view, an organized "awareness" program could substantially increase patent rates and commercial applications.

This argument involved a lengthy string of assumptions. If the results of university research were already well communicated and if useful innovations were already patented, then even if ETIP's effort increased patent rates it would have little or no effect on innovation. In other words, rates of university-based patent applications might not be a realistic measure of technological change. In any case, the short-term increase in patent rates that ETIP achieved may not have reflected any significant shift, but simply a "bulge" as inventors, who would have eventually patented their discoveries anyway, responded to the "awareness" program. In sum, Project 13 was potentially useful, but it was not rigorously designed. Early results may well have been too optimistically interpreted.

In addition to these experiments, the Research and Development Area authored three evaluations (of Projects 7 and 67) and two general studies. The studies, an analysis of demonstration projects by the Rand Corporation (11) and an examination of "federal funding of civilian research and development" by Arthur D. Little, Inc. (19), were implemented in fiscal 1974 and final reports were received in 1976. Another study (48), intended as a follow-up to Project 19, was designed to examine "the management of federal and civilian research and development programs," but the project was scrapped in 1977.

ETIP felt that the study of demonstration projects developed important new "policy guidelines" that would be useful to a number of federal agencies and which could be applied in future policy experiments. Yet, while the Rand Corporation study was well received by several interested agencies, its conclusions seemed rather limited: Demonstration projects were found to be most successful when technological risks were low and when commercial applicability was high. In ETIP's terms, this meant that demonstration projects were best viewed as experiments with the social, cultural, and institutional "field" in which technology transfer would occur. But these findings also seemed nearly self-evident. Demonstration projects may well have been most successful when technological and commercial risks were low, but this is also when they were most likely to be unnecessary.

ETIP's study of federal funding of civilian research and development was intended to be a general examination of R&D policy options. The study's final report concluded that past federal policies had been too little concerned with the coupling of technological development and commercial success. The report further argued that R&D funding was only a small element in industrial innovation. Successful R&D policies should permit industries to make investment decisions while closely watching the private markets in which technological innovations must be accepted. This conclusion, of course, was also a basic assumption underlying ETIP's R&D effort. Unfortunately, the studies' findings were poorly validated. As a detailed investigation of the research process showed (Cohen, 1977), the study provided little more than an ex post facto rationalization for ongoing projects in nearly every ETIP program area.

The theoretical basis for ETIP's R&D activities was formulated early in the program's history. Most R&D projects were already being implemented by the end of fiscal 1974. Although ETIP's hypotheses about the need to coordinate technological and commercial development may well have been valid, the program found it difficult to implement useful experiments that took into account the wide range of technological, social, and institutional factors which were relevant in each particular case. ETIP's general policy prescriptions remained vague observations about the need for agencies to develop R&D planning efforts that took better account of commercialization problems. This was, of course, what most agencies were already trying to do. ETIP never refined its understanding of R&D planning problems much further, nor was it able to specify what R&D funding strategies were appropriate to which circumstances. After the ETIP Evaluation Panel called attention to these problems in its 1975 report, the Research and Development Area was quickly deemphasized.

ADVANCED PLANNING

The final area delineated in ETIP's 1974 Program Plan was Advanced Planning and Research. This area was created to provide an analytical focus for ETIP that would

> selectively conduct and monitor a number of economic and institutional analyses and experiments in order to monitor the progress and orientation of the investigations in the four selected policy areas; . . . explore additional policy areas for ETIP investigation; . . . become familiar with the many programs underway in the mission-oriented federal agencies that are concerned with technological inputs as to possible Federal Government technology policies [ETIP, 1974: 40-41].

In other words, the Advanced Planning and Research Area would help coordinate other ETIP activities by conducting

> analyses and exploratory studies to provide an improved basis for choice of policy questions for future investigation as well as to permit more effective direction and evaluation of the already selected policy areas [ETIP, 1974: 10].

Clearly, the Advanced Planning and Research Area was expected to develop more specific criteria to guide ETIP's selection of projects. By evaluating ongoing projects and by analyzing technology policy options, it was also expected to unify ETIP's diverse efforts and to develop a coordinated theoretical basis for new initiatives.

By July 1976, only two Advanced Planning projects had been developed. One was the transfer of funds through which my own research was supported; the other was an analysis of "Contingency Planning for Anticipated Technological Crises" that was contracted to Charles River Associates. This latter project did produce an interesting study of commodity shortages that considered the economic and political histories, market characteristics, and policy alternatives affecting six potentially critical resources—bauxite, chromite, cobalt, manganese, petroleum, and platinum. In ETIP's words, the emphasis was on

> the development of methodology for evaluating the entire range of alternatives . . . the application of the economic models to short-run policy tools such as stockpiling and import restrictions, and to the long-run measures such as increasing production flexibility through technological substitution [ETIP, 1975: A-54].

Given the continuing threat of political boycotts by commodity cartels, the study attracted wide interest and approval from a range of government agencies. However, it was only peripherally relevant to ETIP's focus on civilian-sector technological change.

Other ETIP program areas fulfilled some of the functions that had been intended for Advanced Planning and Research. Each program area, for example, investigated theoretical issues that were expected to provide the basis for future policy experiments. These in-house studies were rarely very fruitful, however, and never transcended parochial program area interests. Until 1976 each program area was also responsible for developing its own project evaluations. This resulted in a rather uncoordinated set of evaluation studies (Projects 78, 90, 91, 95, and 96) which varied widely in design, sophistication, and rigor. Little effort was made to integrate these studies in order to reach general conclusions about policy alternatives. By fiscal 1977, however, evaluation efforts were shifted to the new Experimental Methods Area.

The Advanced Planning and Research Area did little to refine ETIP's policy hypotheses, program goals, or policy selection criteria. Given the nearly unlimited range of issues and agencies encompassed by ETIP's mandate, this lack of well-defined guidelines made the choice of experiment topics more or less a hit-or-miss proposition. In 1976, however, the Experimental Methods Area began a much more serious effort at developing a comprehensive program framework.

Advanced Planning and Research was also expected to develop channels of communication between ETIP and other private- and public-sector technology programs. While a few "symposia" were organized under the auspices of other program areas (e.g., a Health Products Symposium in conjunction with VA procurement projects), the focus was on project-specific issues. As a result, except for occasional consulting, ETIP has never solicited outside comments, criticism, or information. All in all, the program lacked anything like the overall advanced-planning effort that was initially envisioned.

THE ECONOMIC ASSISTANCE AREA

Economic Assistance was the last ETIP program area to develop, but its goal was basic to the program's mission: "to contribute to technology policy by helping to improve the ability of economic markets to more effectively provide socially desirable technological change" (ETIP, 1977: 1). In fulfilling this goal, the Economic Assistance Area envisioned two rather different project foci: first of all, it intended to investigate economic incentives specifically associated with financial assistance and subsidy policies; second, Economic Assistance expected to develop a broader theoretical framework for all of ETIP's efforts by analyzing the more general relationships among policy alternatives, economic effects, and innovation. In so doing, Economic Assistance would fulfill some of the functions originally intended for Advanced Planning.

The origins of the Economic Assistance Area lay in ETIP's developing interest in federal subsidy policy. After implementing the first set of procurement, regulation, small-business, and R&D projects, ETIP began considering other policy domains that significantly affected technological development. By the winter of 1975, program staff had identified federal subsidies as a major innovation factor:

> Through grants and subsidies the Federal Government provides close to $100 billion annually to state and local governments, utilities, industries, and others for the creation, acquisition, or operation of capital goods. In providing this financial assistance, little thought is given to how it affects technological change [Tassey, 1975].

Although ETIP felt that the magnitude of government subsidies necessarily implied an enormous technological impact, a detailed study was envisioned to gain a better understanding of the precise nature of subsidy effects. Initial plans for such a subsidy study were drafted during the spring of 1975. However, the research guidelines developed in the RFP proved too general, and none of the proposals submitted to ETIP were sufficiently "responsive" to the program's needs. ETIP decided that more in-house research was required.

Although the subsidy study was originally listed as an Advanced Planning activity, by August 1975 progress reports already distinguished a separate Financial Assistance Area. Throughout the fall and winter, in-house research continued, and by the spring of 1976, a new RFP had been written. Soon the first project was under way in what was now being called the Economic Assistance Area.

This study (93) of "federal subsidies and technological change" focused specifically on the role of subsidies in capital formation. Although capital formation subsidies "totalled nearly $20 billion," ETIP argued that it

> had been unable to find evidence of a concerted effort within the Federal Government to systematically analyze these programs and to determine what policy guidelines can be developed for effectively planning, implementing, and managing subsidy programs at the federal, state, and local levels [ETIP, 1976: 27].

Therefore, Project 93 would

> (1) describe and analyze programs involving federal subsidies for capital formation in order to understand how such assistance might be better employed to stimulate, or avoid inhibiting, desirable technological change, and
> (2) identify policy changes that could usefully be tested by ETIP [ETIP, 1976: 27].

A contract to conduct the study was awarded to Charles River Associates in June 1976.

Although the substantive findings of the subsidy research were not yet available in 1977, several aspects of the project's design did raise questions. According to the project plan, the study was investigating the economic impact of alternative subsidy policies. Several issues were being considered: how the results of subsidies could be optimized, how subsidies affected supply and demand, how subsidies affected economic equity, and so on. In essence, the study conducted a detailed economic analysis of past subsidy policies with an eye to future improvements in subsidy effectiveness. In ETIP's view, this kind of general framework was required because

> technological change must be analyzed in terms of its contribution to desirable capital formation and therefore efficient economic growth. Thus a broad economic analysis is required in order to place innovation policy in its proper context with respect to overall micro-economic policy [Tassey, 1975].

Still, technological change was rarely the explicit goal of federal subsidies, which were usually directed at more general social benefits. Technological change occurred, at best, as a by-product of most subsidy programs, as a means to some other end. Thus, ETIP's study of the economic effects of subsidies was much more relevant to improving subsidy policy, as such, than to stimulating technological change. Indeed, the project plan emphasized the importance of understanding a wide range of nontechnological effects of subsidy alternatives.

Still, it was certainly true that ETIP as a whole had a pressing need for an improved capability in economic analysis. Regulation, procurement, and subsidy all influenced technological development by altering the economic environment in which private-sector decisions were made. A thorough understanding of the economic effects of policy alternatives was a necessary basis for effective program-planning and action. In its early days, ETIP made little attempt to seriously investigate the microeconomic effects of policies affecting technological change. This was a void that the Economic Assistance Area soon sought to fill.

By the summer of 1975, the Economic Assistance Area Already envisioned studies that would help develop specific guidelines

> for determining when financial assistance should be provided in lieu of regulation . . . in conjunction with regulation . . . in conjunction

with incentive type procurement policies . . . for coordinating Federal R&D sponsorship and financial assistance programs [ETIP, 1975:
6].

By the summer of 1976, Economic Assistance had absorbed a
number of ongoing ETIP studies into a thorough appraisal of
the economic impact of policy alternatives. The goal was to
develop a "prototype for a more systematic and effective
approach to developing micro-economic policy in other [ETIP]
policy areas" (ETIP 1977: 7). As the 1977 Economic Assistance
Area Plan carefully emphasized, effective manipulation of economic incentives should not place undue emphasis on any single
policy tool (such as procurement, regulation, or subsidy). ETIP
needed to determine not only when intervention was required,
but what kind of policy change was most appropriate. In
answering this question. Economic Assistance sought to bolster
ETIP's underlying theoretical rationale and to provide a much-
needed integration of program activities.

By the spring of 1977, the Economic Assistance Area had
added two staff members and was developing several new projects. An experiment (145) using federal subsidies to promote
solar energy development was being negotiated, as well as an
experimental follow-up to the Research and Development
Area's earlier venture capital study. These efforts became side-
tracked, however, after ETIP was reviewed and restructured in
1977.

After ETIP's Research and Development and Small Business
Areas were deemphasized in 1976, the Economic Assistance
Area assumed responsibility for a number of ongoing experiments and studies. In addition to its own subsidy project (93),
Economic Assistance began managing the Connecticut Product
Development Corporation projects (32, 78, and 79), the Technological Competency Evaluations for the SBA (46), and the
studies of critical commodity shortages (17, 132, and 135) and
venture capital markets (11). Several of these projects involved
economic issues that cross-cut program areas responsibilities.
Still, the Economic Assistance Area did not see program liaison
as its responsibility. Without clear substantive links to other
program elements, Economic Assistance developed a general

approach to economic analysis that lacked any specifically technological focus. By 1977, this shift away from technology policy had also become characteristic of other program areas and, especially, of Experimental Methods.

EXPERIMENTAL METHODS

According to the 1974 Program Plan, project design and evaluation was the responsibility of ETIP's Advanced Planning Area and of individual program areas. As we have seen, the Advanced Planning Area was never able to fulfill its evaluation role, while the sophistication of the evaluations conducted by individual program areas varied greatly. During the summer of 1975, ETIP therefore hired a new evaluation manager to coordinate project assessments. This concern for project evaluation was soon translated into a more general "experimental methods" initiative.

ETIP's evaluations were never intended to be limited to assessments of individual projects. The program needed guidance concerning the general principles and policies that its projects could and should address. Evaluations were expected to provide the basis for refining program guidelines and clarifying project selection criteria. As a result, the Experimental Methods Area sought to serve two major functions: to help design and evaluate specific projects, and to develop a better understanding of the program as a whole.

Before the Experimental Methods Area was formed, project evaluations ranged from a $10,000 "real-time case history" (96) of the Integrated Utility Systems project, to a multihundred thousand dollar appraisal (78) of the Connecticut Product Development Corporation. ETIP worried that such a diversity of evaluations would preclude meaningful comparisons and lack credibility.

When an evaluation manager was hired in 1975, the first task was developing an overall framework for evaluating ETIP's procurement activities. Several procurement experiments had already been implemented and data were needed to facilitate the design of follow-ups. The Experimental Methods Area quickly assumed responsibility for two existing procurement evaluations and began developing a general system for evaluating all of ETIP's procurement efforts.

First, the problems posed by these procurement evaluations had to be clarified. Experimental Methods considered three separate evaluation projects: one to assess the agency impact of procurement projects during the period of active implementation; a second to assess the commercial impact of procurement projects during both their experimental and their postexperimental phases; and a third to evaluate postexperimental agency impacts.

After some modification, two major procurement evaluations (Projects 120 and 121) were implemented during the spring of 1976 at a total cost of about $1.6 million. One of these projects assessed the agency impact and the other the commercial impact of FSS procurement experiments. Together, the projects were expected to form the basis for an evaluation system that would consider all of ETIP's procurement activities at all cooperating agencies. The initial evaluations would themselves last for several years and would consider all three cycles of ETIP/FSS procurement. To complement these large investigations, the Experimental Methods Area also commissioned several small-scale case studies of experiment implementation.

The Experimental Methods Area's second major effort was to help in the design of the postmarketing surveillance project (88) with the Food and Drug Administration. The goal was to make the project more easily evaluable from the start by incorporating controlled comparions of alternative drug surveillance methods into the initial design. Yet, as we have already discussed, the project's most significant problem was not an inadequate experimental design, but a limited relevance to technological change. Moreover, the cost of the FDA project was extremely high: Including an eventual evaluation, nearly a million and a half dollars were budgeted.

In addition to its work on individual evaluations and designs, the Experimental Methods Area also sought to develop a better understanding of ETIP's broader contribution. It analyzed policy findings and procedures in each program area and critically assessed both failures and successes to determine the nature of underlying issues and needs. As the first step toward improving overall program-planning, the Experimental Methods Area delineated six stages in the process through which ETIP (1976: 31) investigated policy questions:

(1) problem area identification
(2) problem delineation
(3) project design
(4) project plan
(5) project implementation
(6) project evaluation

According to the Experimental Methods model, ETIP initiated project development by considering general interest areas and identifying relevant federal agencies. Next, specific agencies were contacted and asked to help define policy-related problems, design a project, and write a project plan. During and after project implementation, an evaluation would be conducted "to describe what happens during the course of the project, and to describe the impact of the project on the agency and the economy" (ETIP, 1976: 32-33). If indicated, project follow-ups would then be pursued, leading eventually to broader policy change recommendations.

This is certainly a rather idealized description of the "ETIP process." Yet the Experimental Methods Area used this "model" to formulate guidelines for the execution of ETIP's tasks. Not unexpectedly, this involved a description of existing ETIP procedures more than an analysis of program needs. In the Experimental Methods Area's view, "ETIP is still in a learning mode. Its tasks and breadth of scope are relatively unusual for a federal agency; consequently, to date no firm guidelines for executing the six tasks have been established" (ETIP, 1976: 32-33). In the matter of problem area identification, for example, we learned that "contractors cannot be relied upon because they are not as sensitive to pragmatic agency and policy goals and constraints which must guide ETIP's behavior" (ETIP, 1976: 3). No criteria were provided for selecting problems for investigation. No theoretical issues were defined. Yet, it was just this absence of clear problem definitions that resulted in ETIP's lack of overall program coherence.

The Experimental Methods Area's other conclusions about the ETIP process were also little more than analytical descriptions of options faced. We learn, for example, that in the project design stage, ETIP decided whether to conduct a study, an experiment design, or an experiment, and that the program always needed to keep future evaluation needs in mind. Similarly, we are told that "a variety of approaches have been attempted" in "project implementation"; that "contractors have played a major role" in studies; that lead-agency responsibility for experiments will be assumed by either a contractor, an agency, or ETIP; and that while no evaluations have yet been completed, a greater rigor is expected in the future. Only in the area of problem definition is there an attempt to define more specific guidelines for program actions:

A consensus is developing within ETIP concerning the following problem selection criteria:

(1) addresses high-priority national need (e.g., energy, health care, environment);
(2) sufficiently broad scope to be generic but not so broad as to be impractical;
(3) high-level agency commitment . . . ;
(4) clearly adds to ETIP's knowledge base . . . or established important growth direction for ETIP;
(5) avoid policy areas dominated by political decision-making (e.g., taxation);
(6) experiments should be clearly evaluable;
(7) ripeness;
(8) identifiability of ETIP contributions [ETIP, 1976: 33].

Yet even these criteria remain much too general and subjective to provide effective guidance for program action.

All along, ETIP's most difficult task was to delineate relevant policy hypotheses and to translate them into effective projects. The program faced an extremely wide range of project options, but lacked explicit criteria to guide the selection of some policy areas, policy tools, and policy impacts over others. The recommendation that ETIP address "high-priority national needs" was insufficient without a better understanding of how such needs could be identified. Nowhere in the Experimental Methods Area's list of priorities was there any mention of ETIP's technological mission. Perhaps it was simply assumed that ETIP staff understood the program's purpose well enough. But the program's technological mandate remained undefined.

This was, of course, ETIP's first attempt to develop a more rigorous analytic framework, and the Experimental Methods Area was well aware that more work was needed. A list of "improvements to be made in the ETIP process" was developed.

(1) improved project selection criteria.
(2) Evaluation designs will become an integral part of all relevant project plans.
(3) The role of studies will be carefully defined and the conditions under which they are used more clearly specified.
(4) A systematic procedure for evaluating ETIP's project selection, implementation and evaluation process will be established . . . :

   A. Given ETIP's objectives, what project selection procedures are appropriate?
   B. Given ETIP's objects and contraints, when are specific types of project implementation strategies appropriate?
   C. What types of evaluation strategies are appropriate for ETIP's goals and constraints?

(5) An informal process for using outside project opportunity reviewers will be established [ETIP, 1976: 35] .

These suggestions did provide a reasonable starting point for improvements.

However, the Experimental Methods Area's [1976: 36) assessment of the "need for ETIP" was a bit more problematic:

ETIP currently is addressing three needs which apparently are not being satisfied by existing federal programs. . . . Firstly, ETIP provides a multi-agency focus for policy problems. . . . Secondly, ETIP operates as a catalyst for change . . . with respect to a variety of policy problems. . . . A third need . . . concerns setting standards for policy experimentation and evaluation. . . . ETIP is in a position to set standards for the conduct of experiments and evaluations. . . . In sum, ETIP is a force addressing substantive multi-agency problems

and facilitating policy changes. By actively supporting the use of
policy experimentation, it is also working to improve the policy-
making methodologies used by agencies.

Nowhere was there any reference to technology, technology
policy, or better ways of facilitating innovation. Instead, ETIP's
purpose was simply to improve the selection of "policy alternatives" by agencies. This was accomplished through a "multi-
agency focus" (although most projects involved a single partner)
and through ETIP's commitment to experimental testing.
Rather than creating an appropriate environment for technological change, ETIP's goal had now become improving the
efficiency of government—both policy selection procedures and
the effectiveness of chosen policies.

The experimental testing of public policies may be a widely
applicable tool, but the encouragement of policy experimentation was not ETIP's mandated mission. Indeed, the topic of
policy experimentation covers a range of issues and interests
that is much too broad for a program like ETIP to cope with
effectively. Still, ETIP's growing interest in general policy
assessment, its increased funding of evaluations, and its selection of projects bearing little relevance to technological change
all indicated a significant shift in the program's conception.

The Experimental Methods Area tried to fulfill an extremely
important function by developing a more rigorous overall
framework for the design and evaluation of ETIP projects. But
this was not an easy function to fullfill. ETIP's strategy of
stimulating innovation through policy experiments was
extremely broad in scope. And while few ETIP projects focused
solely on technological change, over time experiments began
increasingly to emphasize other kinds of social and economic
benefits. The Experimental Methods Area further articulated
this shift by delineating ETIP's purpose as a general attempt to
improve public policies. The reasons for this shift, and its
broader implications, will become clearer as we analyze the
dynamics of project implementation and bureaucratic life.

Chapter 6

PROGRAM DYNAMICS

ETIP was not created in a single instant or in a series of rational, mechanical steps. The ideas embodied in the 1974 Program Plan were tested in action. Goals were interpreted, theories modified, and procedures adjusted to meet the practical needs of program implementation. Over time, everyday program activities began reflecting the personal understandings of staff, the pressures from ETIP's larger organizational environment, and the program's underlying search for bureaucratic survival.

ETIP changed markedly during its first three years of operation. By 1977, only two of ETIP's original five policy areas were left, and two new program areas had been developed. Almost all of the initial staff were gone, but the total number of program professionals had nearly doubled from seven to twelve. The project list had grown to more than 150 titles, of which more than half were inactive. Policy experiments had proven much more difficult to develop than anticipated, and an increasing emphasis was being placed on policy studies. Most important, ETIP's theoretical focus had shifted sharply, reflecting basic changes in the program's underlying assumptions, hypotheses, and goals.

In response both to internal problems and external pressures, ETIP developed informal organizational patterns that redefined the character of program activities. By examining the nature of this informal organization, we can better understand what kind of program ETIP became and how and why it developed.

ETIP'S ORGANIZATIONAL ENVIRONMENT[1]

Any understanding of ETIP's evolution must begin with an examination of ETIP's place in the federal bureaucracy. ETIP was located at the National Bureau of Standards, which is itself a part of the Department of Commerce. The program's relationship with both of these larger organizations strongly influenced its activities and development.

ETIP's physical location was a suite of offices on the seventh floor of the National Bureau of Standard's administration building in Gaithersburg, Maryland. This was, of course, only a part-time home for most of ETIP's professional staff, since the business of negotiating contracts and managing projects took place all over Washington and the country. As one of the program's managers noted, "ETIP proper is just rented office space . . . a place where there are phones and secretaries and a hook to hang your hat. It's the nerve center, the paperwork and phone call center, but most of my important business—my meetings, conferences, and presentations—take place elsewhere." ETIP's immediate supervisors were found at the Bureau, and Bureau administrators reviewed all of ETIP's projects and "signed off" on all contracts and fund transfers.

ETIP was officially part of the NBS director's office. This was a rather unusual location, somewhat outside the regular "table of organization." Then again, ETIP was a rather unusual program, one that had been imposed on the Bureau by presidential mandate. Unlike most Bureau programs, ETIP had no direct involvement in hard scientific research. NBS administrators saw ETIP as a "soft" program. They worried that it was too concerned with self-aggrandizement and public relations. They were concerned about ETIP's optimistic press releases, its blatant lobbying, and its direct contacts with the White House. They feared that some of ETIP's more controversial projects might eventually become sources of embarrassment.

NBS may have wanted ETIP to be a better "scientist," but the Department of Commerce was more concerned with action. DoC kept a much closer watch on ETIP than on more traditional branches of the Bureau. At least in theory, all ETIP projects received final approval from the Assistant Secretary of Commerce for Science and Technology.

Despite the delays in ETIP's start-up, the Department of Commerce wanted projects to begin quickly. DoC did not view ETIP as a detached policy analyst, but rather as an agent of policy change. ETIP was under constant pressure to demonstrate that it had stimulated the development and commercialization of useful technology or that it had otherwise fulfilled DoC's broader economic goals.

None of these pressures would have posed a serious problem if ETIP's funding had been more certain. ETIP, however, was a new program, and it was clearly labeled "experimental." By 1974, ERDIP, a related program at the National Science Foundation, had already been scrapped. During ETIP's first few years, there were several times when the program's demise appeared imminent. In any case, it was well understood that ETIP's accomplishments would be thoroughly reviewed no later than 1980, at which time a decision about the program's future would be made.

ETIP's insecurity was compounded by the program's lack of a clearly defined outside constituency. At times, ETIP viewed its National Academy of Science Evaluation Panel members as influential, high-level program advocates. But when these panel members began asking tough questions, ETIP realized that they were not only advisers and supporters, but reviewers and critics as well. As a result, ETIP began exploring other possible sources of program backing.

Since most of the public had little interest in technology, ETIP's press releases began emphasizing the cost savings and efficiency that resulted from the program's initiatives. Program staff began speaking to press clubs, industry associations, and public interest groups. Descriptions of ETIP's accomplishments were sent to relevant congressional committees. By 1976, ETIP had begun consulting for the White House staff. Soon, however, letters and editorials in the scientific press began raising questions about ETIP's claims. Eventually, the Department of Commerce became concerned. ETIP's director was finally told that lobbying for his own program was inappropriate and that outside "consulting" had to be approved through proper bureaucratic channels.

Because of continuing doubts about ETIP's "usefulness" and "scientific value," the program sought to demonstrate its worth through highly "visible" projects, leading at times to unwise project choices. DoC's interest in practical value was not always consonant with NBS's concern for scientific rigor. ETIP's director began viewing "politics" as an increasingly important part of his role and a concern for the substance of program activities was increasingly replaced by a concern for the appearance of project success. It is thus not surprising that ETIP often vacillated in its emphasis between "scientific knowledge" and "practical achievements."

ETIP's ambivalence was also indicated by continuing changes in the program's emphasis from technological innovation to social benefits, government efficiency, and experimental methods. These shifts were most strongly influenced by the final major element in ETIP's organizational environment—the agencies with which the program cooperated. Few agencies were interested in policies aimed solely at private-sector technological results. Unless agencies perceived more direct benefits, ETIP's willingness to provide expertise, to fund exceptional costs, and to assume risks was meaningless. Combined with other environmental pressures, ETIP's pressing need for agency cooperation had a profound effect on the nature of program operations.

PROGRAM OPERATIONS

Not too surprisingly, ETIP's plans and ETIP's actions were never entirely congruent. Although the program was ideologically committed to policy manipulation, most of its projects have been passive policy studies. Originally, ETIP expected to base its actions on clearly delineated theories about public policy and innovation, which would yield specific hypotheses that agencies would be eager to test. In fact, existing innovation theory proved much weaker than ETIP anticipated, and, in any case, agencies proved to have little concern about the impact of their actions on civilian technological development. As a result, ETIP was forced to seek a more pragmatic basis for agency cooperation.

According to ETIP's formal guidelines, the development of experimental projects was relatively straightforward. ETIP began by conducting the minimal amount of background research necessary to identify clearly validated relationships between public policies and technological change. These theoretical propositions were then translated into specific policy change hypotheses. Responsible agencies were contacted and experimental tests were naturally developed.

Reality, however, was not so simple. The relationships between public policies and technology were not always clear-cut, and a substantial portion of ETIP's resources were invested in basic policy research. Just as important, the process of experiment development proved to involve much more than the simple transfer of ETIP-developed hypotheses to agency settings. The result was a rather different set of program operations than ETIP had originally envisioned.

ETIP Studies

According to the 1974 Program Plan, abstract studies would be a relatively minor aspect of ETIP operations. The Program Plan assumed that the theoretical basis for most of ETIP's policy experiments could be easily identified from the existing literature. Indeed, several possible policy experiments were already described in the Program Plan itself. ETIP's Advanced Planning Area was expected to conduct those few studies that would be needed to identify new policy issues for experimentation. ETIP's substantive program areas were seen as active interveners that would initiate actual policy tests.

In fact, ETIP found it extremely difficult to translate policy examples into actual policy experiments. As a result, all of the program areas began funding a wide range of background studies. Some of these studies focused explicitly on the design of future experiments. Other general studies aimed at more basic policy research, analyzing topics such as the technological impact of government purchasing, the relationship between federal funding and civilian R&D, or the economics of federal subsidy. In addition, a number of projects that ETIP labeled "experiments" consisted, for the most part, of contracted analytical studies. By 1976, ETIP's investment in evaluation studies was also rapidly increasing. The result was that well over half of ETIP's projects focused on some aspect of passive policy research.

Studies managed by ETIP itself (those that were not part of some larger cooperative experiment), usually began with background research by relevant staff members. The choice of subject matter derived from a number of sources: (preliminary) literature reviews, staff discussions, external requests, or, as was often the case, suggestions by the program director. Even this initial background research was sometimes contracted to "expert" consultants through "sole-source" agreements. In any case, when successful, the results of such research were translated into a preliminary "project plan" which defined the area to be studied and its relationship to ETIP's broader technology and policy interests.

This preliminary project plan was circulated for staff comments before being presented in a formal draft to ETIP's director. The director checked to see that the proposal was consistent with ETIP's general purpose and with his earlier perception of what was being developed. Next, the project plan was sent "upstairs" for formal approval by the National Bureau of Standards hierarchy. It went first to the NBS legal and procurement offices and then to the associate and deputy directors for operations, who recommended action by the Bureau director. Until March of 1975, approval by the Assistant Secretary of Commerce for Science and Technology was also necessary. The whole approval process (expedited by ETIP's administrative assistant) usually took from two to three weeks. The outcome was a formal project plan ready to be translated into a request for proposals (RFP).

Information about ETIP's general goals, selection criteria, and so on, were added when staff prepared the RFP. If a sole-source contract was envisioned, this procedure was justified and terms negotiated at this stage. In any case, once the RFP was drafted, it was again turned over to the NBS and DoC procurement offices, where it was reviewed for completeness and accuracy. At least in theory, the RFP could be rejected anywhere along the line. In practice, revisions were sometimes suggested, but only one of ETIP's proposed projects was ever formally rejected at this stage.

Contracts for studies were normally awarded through an open competition. Within about two weeks of the RFP's approval, a contract negotiator was appointed from outside the program. With ETIP's help, the negotiator drafted an announcement for prospective bidders that was published in the *Commerce Business Daily* and also circulated directly to relevant firms. Thirty days were generally allowed for responses. Proposals were sent directly to the Department of Commerce, which ranked them high to low in terms of cost.

ETIP had its own procedures for evaluating proposals, a process that involved three separate proposal submissions. The first proposal, which was evaluated without the contractor being identified, focused on the firm's conceptualization of the research topic. The second proposal was concerned with administrative qualifications—how the firm was managed and how it would manage this particular project. The final proposal included a specific breakdown of project tasks and costs. Sometimes, for highly technical topics, ETIP adopted a formal two-step contracting procedure in which potential bidders were invited to a preliminary conference at which ETIP's understanding of the issues was discussed.

After ETIP received the proposals, it appointed a panel of government employees (including ETIP staff) to review them. After considering all the proposals, the review panel usually selected one to four of the submissions as "most responsive." The negotiator then contacted these prospective contractors and scheduled a meeting with ETIP staff to discuss remaining ambiguities and issues. Afterwards, each contractor submitted a "best and final" offer. One was selected and the contract awarded.

The whole process took about six months. Sometimes, as in the case of ETIP's subsidy study (93), none of the initial submissions was judged to be sufficiently responsive. If ETIP wanted to continue, more background research would be conducted, a more explicit project plan written, and the selection process begun anew.

Once a contract was signed, an appropriate ETIP staff member assumed responsibility for monitoring the study's progress. This involved meeting with the contractor, reviewing project reports, and, in many cases, coordinating supplementary consulting services. If, as often happened, the project fell behind schedule, or if ETIP became dissatisfied with results, the manager's work could be very time-consuming. When an acceptable final report was eventually received, the study was completed.

By 1977, several ETIP studies had been finished and a number of others were nearly done. The experience demonstrated well both the values and the limitations of consultancy research. Most of ETIP's experiment design studies, for example, proved unusable. The plans that were produced for Veterans Administration procurement experiments (39) and for regulatory experiments (44 and 45) were simply unrealistic. In ETIP's view, contractors were insufficiently sensitive to program and agency needs. As a result, ETIP stopped funding new experiment design studies by mid-1975. Instead, experiments were developed "in-house," in combination with agency partners and with the help of more general studies of policy alternatives.

Although some of ETIP's general studies (for example, Booz-Allen's research on government procurement) proved quite useful in the development of policy experiments, most were simply broad analytical reviews of major policy areas. While ETIP's analyses of critical commodity shortages (11), alternative pesticide systems (8), federal funding of civilian R&D (19), or federal demonstration projects (9) might add to our theoretical knowledge of important policy arenas, they had little immediate relevance to the development of policy experiments.

Indeed, the value of such consultancy research could be questioned at an even more basic level. A detailed review of ETIP's study of federal funding of civilian R&D (Cohen, 1977), for example, revealed a research process of less than complete rigor. Right from the start, ETIP's contractor selection procedures placed heavy emphasis on identifying firms that were sufficiently "sensitive" to ETIP's views—that is, which saw federal R&D support as a relatively minor component in innovation. In analyzing data from case studies of six industrial sectors, the contractor progressively, and subjectively, distilled findings to underemphasize the role that R&D played. Not surprisingly, the study's conclusions strongly supported ETIP's view that commercialization, not R&D support, was the critical innovation issue. Indeed, ETIP was already funding projects based on this premise well before the research results were in.

Similar comments could be made about many of ETIP's other studies, or, for that matter, about consultancy research at other agencies (see, for example, Vivelo, 1980). It is not surprising that agencies holding strong policy viewpoints hire contractors that share these views. Nor is it surprising that such contractors honestly interpret their data in expected ways. The result is that most consultancy research itself becomes part of the politics (rather than the science) of policy debate. Indeed, this problem has been the source of much of the recent controversy over the excessive use of consultants by government agencies. Consultancy research may be an effective method for agencies to spend end-of-year funds—and no agency wants to be left with a surplus—but the results are often of limited utility.

In this regard, ETIP's contracted studies were probably of higher quality than those of most agencies. ETIP's analysis of demonstration projects, critical commodity shortages, and venture capital markets, for example, attracted widely favorable notice. However, it is also true that such policy studies are much easier to develop than policy experiments, and that in each of its first two years, ETIP was left with nearly a million dollars in unspent funds. It is no wonder that, over time, a larger and larger proportion of ETIP's budget was spent on bigger and bigger studies and on experiments that contained substantial components of basic policy research.

By 1976, ETIP had begun a new series of evaluation studies that were expected to require an increasing share of program resources. The first series of procurement evaluations, for example, were funded at well over a million dollars—more than one-third of the program's annual budget. Although such evaluations may be a necessary part of policy experimentation, their value was unproved. By 1977, ETIP was investing an ever-increasing portion of its resources in such analytical studies. It was beginning to look more and more like any other research-oriented government program.

ETIP Experiments

ETIP originally expected that developing and implementing policy experiments would be relatively easy. Projects would be based on clearly delineated theories about public policy and innovation. Once relevant agencies were contacted and the valued of the experiments explained, agency cooperation would be assured. However, most agencies proved to have little interest in policy experiments aimed at stimulating technological change.

ETIP's most basic need was for agency trust and support and, as a result, most ETIP experiments developed rather differently from what had been formally planned. In practice, ETIP rarely initiated an experiment by analyzing abstract theory or constructing rigorous hypotheses, but instead by establishing agency contacts. These contacts could derive from personal friendships (one project, for example, grew out of conversations in a car pool), from professional relationships, or even from formal presentations in which ETIP promoted its past accomplishments. Once contact was established, an effort was made to understand how agencies perceived their problems, and to formulate projects that addressed them. Project "champions" were sought who would support ETIP efforts within their agencies and identify their own concerns with them.

Agencies agreed to participate in ETIP projects for a variety of reasons. Sometimes they were under external pressure to improve efficiency, but lacked the authority or expertise to alter policies on their own accord. ETIP then became a convenient resource. The implementation of a cooperative project demonstrated that the agency was "doing something." If the project failed, ETIP could shoulder the blame.

Even if a project held little relevance to agency goals, some agency staff members might still find the project in their personal interest. By identifying with an ETIP initiative, a person might advance his or her career or political power within the agency. Interestingly enough, the availability of ETIP funding was rarely a sufficient reason for agency cooperation. Indeed, ETIP sometimes found itself in the awkward position of "selling" money to agencies that already had difficulty spending their own. The situation was different, however, when the use of agency funds was restricted. The Food and Drug Administration (88), for example, had extremely limited resources for policy research. In this case, the availability of ETIP funding was an extremely strong selling point.

When ETIP and agency goals were at least partially congruent, projects could be developed that met mutual needs. ETIP and the Federal Supply Service, for example, had different but complementary interests in life cycle costing. ETIP, perhaps too optimistically, anticipated that new government purchasing practices would stimulate the development of more energy-efficient appliances. FSS saw these same new procedures as the source of both substantial government cost savings and improved appliance performance.

Still, there were few situations where such a clear complementarity of interests could be found. Projects often seemed much more concerned with solving agency problems than with ETIP's own interest in technological development. The reasons for this are clear; ETIP was under enormous pressure to develop projects and allocate funds. Existing theories about public policy and innovation were weak and poorly defined. In the area of regulation, for example, this policy theory could be loosely interpreted to mean little more than the need to "free the market" or "improve agency efficiency"–"hypotheses" to which nearly any agency concern could be related. At the same time, ETIP was left with nearly a million dollars in unspent funds after each of its first two years. Within the federal government, this is clear evidence that something is wrong. Given the program's need to spend funds, it was not surprising that ETIP sometimes compromised its technology goals to develop "useful" projects concerned with "newsworthy" topics, such as energy, drugs, or occupational safety.

ETIP's cooperative experiments were implemented somewhat differently from its analytical studies, even when the ultimate result was a similar kind of passive policy research. From ETIP's point of view, experiments did not involve any direct responsibility for contractors or RFPs. After many meetings and discussions, ETIP or agency staff would finally begin preparing a project plan. Drafts of this plan could be circulated, commented on, revised, and recirculated for several months before final agreement was reached.

Project funding would also be negotiated at this time, but, as we have seen, this was rarely a major source of ETIP-agency conflict. When necessary, ETIP was willing to spend freely for a project, once agency cooperation was assured. As a result, the amount of a project's funding was not necessarily very closely related to ETIP's judgment of the project's importance as a test of technology policy issues. Indeed, over time, ETIP tended to develop more expensive projects, as well as new program areas (such as Experimental Methods) that were better able to spend funds.

ETIP generally paid only for the "exceptional" costs involved in implementing a project. This included, for example, the extra cost for new kinds of performance-testing in procurement projects, but not the purchases of new products themselves. ETIP's contribution also often included all or part of the cost of an experiment's contracted studies, the cost of hiring consultants, or the administrative expenses resulting from new procedures. Usually, at least some financial commitment was expected from the cooperating agency. This often took the form of staff time, with agency personnel handling day-to-day project management, while ETIP monitored overall progress.

ETIP-agency negotiations culminated in a formal project plan that specified the details of ETIP, agency, and contractor responsibilities—arrangements for fund transfers, contractor selection, and project management and monitoring. An important part of this project plan was the "work statement" which delineated project hypotheses, the tasks the project would carry out, and the "milestones" for project achievements. Once successfully negotiated, this project plan went through the same kind of NBS approval as a project plan for a study. However, as soon as approval was received, the experiment was ready for implementation without any complicated RFP procedure on ETIP's part. At this point, ETIP funds could be transferred directly to the cooperating agency through an advance, a reimbursement for costs, and so on.

After funds were transferred, problems and complications could still occur. When an experiment included a policy study, for example, the agency usually assumed primary responsibility for contractor selection, but ETIP expected to play an important role in writing the RFP and evaluating responses. Sometimes, differences emerged between ETIP and agency perceptions of the precise nature of the work to be done or the best qualified people to do it. ETIP also became concerned when projects fell behind schedule or when, in ETIP's view, an agency began to reinterpret a project's emphasis or scope. Once an experiment began, such problems were usually resolved through negotiations, and often through ETIP compromises. Given ETIP's dependence on agency cooperation, the program was rarely willing to put a project on the line (for example, by cutting off funds), even when serious differences emerged.

After experiments were initiated, pressures for change could come from a variety of sources: congressional scrutiny, agency politics, advocacy groups, or changing ETIP priorities. In any case, even after policy changes were implemented, results still had to be evaluated and recommendations for future action made. No ETIP projects had reached this final stage when intensive field research ended in 1977.

Several ETIP experiments involved little more than fund transfers to support agency-contracted analytical studies. In our terms, such projects have, in fact, been labeled "studies." However, a number of other ETIP projects that incorporate policy studies, but which also include eventual plans for policy-testing (e.g., the FRA reefer study, 32), have been labeled "experiments." Even so, only about 30 percent of ETIP's projects involved any kind of policy change. Clearly designed policy experiments represent only a handful of ETIP's efforts.

PROGRAM AREA DIFFERENCES

By the fall of 1973, ETIP had developed a basic theoretical framework for its investigation of public policy and innovation. It had focused on a broad range of government actions that indirectly influenced the social and economic framework for innovation decision-making. It had formulated several specific hypotheses about the effects of various policy changes on technological development. It had delineated internal program areas that were related to agency responsibilities in procurement, regulation, small business, and research and development. It had codified preliminary ideas into a formal program plan.

In 1974, ETIP began implementing its first projects. While the program tried to maintain some relevance to innovation, it quickly learned that most agencies were much more concerned about their own internal problems. ETIP also discovered that the rigorous technology policy "theory" that it expected to apply often amounted to little more than current political wisdom. Faced with strong pressures to act, the program began seeking "targets of opportunity," continually balancing its concern for innovation against agency desires. The outcome was a substantial shift in program activities, and a process of accommodation that varied from program area to program area.

Eventually, ETIP's informal organization, formal structure, and underlying goals were significantly altered.

In many ways, ETIP's Procurement Area faced the fewest problems. The same procurement techniques needed to stimulate innovation could also increase agency efficiency. The Federal Supply Service was not interested in life cycle costing because it would stimulate innovation, but because it would save money. Indeed, since the FSS did not itself use the products purchased, it also had little interest in product performance. As a result, ETIP's attempts to include product performance criteria other than energy costing (for example, the attempt to purchase quieter lawn mowers) were unsuccessful. Eventually, ETIP established an Experimental Technology Office at FSS is an effort to increase agency interest in technological improvement. In a sense, ETIP was seeking to establish a stronger internal agency champion. But this single new office had little effect on the FSS bureaucracy. When ETIP created a similar technology office at the Veterans Administration, the results were even more disappointing.

Over time, the Procurement Area's development of new projects slowed. Later projects, moreover, placed less emphasis on searching for "better ways" of stimulating innovation and concentrated more and more on procurement effectiveness. This was reflected both in ETIP's press releases, which emphasized cost savings and government efficiency, and in formal project descriptions. The potential for mutual benefits was overshadowed by ETIP's desire to develop projects as quickly and successfully as possible.

Most regulatory agencies had even less interest in technological innovation than procurement offices. Regulatory responsibilities, moreover, were administratively dispersed in scores of agencies. As a result, ETIP found it difficult to develop regulatory experiments that had clear technological relevance. Although several projects were started quickly, progress soon slowed. Early studies provided only vague guidelines that proved to be little help in experiment design. ETIP's regulatory staff continued searching for a pragmatic basis for agency cooperation, and several different implementation strategies were tried. Instead of working directly with agencies, for example, some ETIP projects focused on interested parties to regulatory decisions. Others concentrated on abstract economic analysis that had little direct bearing on policy change.

ETIP's underlying problem was the weakness of the policy theory that could be applied. Most of ETIP's regulatory efforts were based on the rather simple premise that regulation altered "free market" norms and artificially biased investment from technological development. But regulation necessarily alters market realities—for example, to protect the public from natural monopolies. Moreover, the market biases imposed by regulation do not necessarily hinder innovation, but can, as has historically been the case with communications technology, just as easily stimulate it. What is "natural" is not necessarily best; regulations could be designed to encourage just about any level of technological investment desired.

In theory, more accurate economic analysis could enable regulators to fine-tune economic incentives toward a range of socially desired goals. ETIP's experiments with regulatory rates were not, however, that sophisticated. In many cases, the policy changes that ETIP implemented seemed little more than thin rationalizations for higher industry profits.

In other regulatory areas, the potential for mutually beneficial policy experiments seemed greater. Improved efficiency in new product certification, for example, could be directly tied to technological change. By emphasizing agency-perceived bottlenecks, such projects also courted agency cooperation. But, over time, ETIP's Regulatory Area overemphasized its role as an agency problem solver. Later projects showed little, if any, concern for technological development. Even more than in procurement, ETIP's Regulatory Area became an advocate for agency interests and the diffuse public benefits of regulatory reform.

ETIP's Small Business Area was originally intended to support inventors and small firms which have been important past sources of technological change. Indeed, ETIP's earliest small-business projects focused directly on innovation—for example, through the patent awareness program. However, later projects sought to develop a stronger institutional base in the Small Business Administration. ETIP helped the SBA evaluate technological issues, such as regulatory compliance, that affected small businesses. Unfortunately, none of the SBA projects was a true experiment, and the SBA showed little interest in technological change as such. Since few important areas for cooperation existed, ETIP's Small Business Area was deemphasized and became virtually defunct.

ETIP's Research and Development Area also developed a number of studies and experiments quickly, but new projects were again slow to emerge. ETIP was unable to develop clearly defined policy hypotheses that could be tested in a range of R&D settings. The commercialization issues that ETIP did emphasize were usually product-specific. In any case, most R&D agencies were already aware of the importance of considering eventual commercial development. The Research and Development Area initially sought to establish a role as a consultant to R&D funding agencies, but after implementing one experiment and a few studies, ETIP's interest petered out.

By 1977, ETIP's Advanced Planning, Economic Assistance, and Experimental Methods areas had not yet implemented any experiments. Although the Advanced Planning Area funded one study, it was never able to fulfill its planning and coordination function. The Economic Assistance Area was formed in 1976 as a locus for ETIP's interest in federal subsidy and began implementing its first major study in 1977. By then, this area had also begun investigating underlying issues in economic theory that could provide the basis for more rigorous policy change hypotheses for the program as a whole. However, the most striking change in ETIP's operations was the emergence of the Experimental Methods Area, which was responsible for project evaluation and for assisting other ETIP areas in project design. By 1977, ETIP was increasingly emphasizing its role as an "experimental methodologist." In less than a year, the Experimental Methods Area had expanded to four professionals who were spending more than one-third of the program's budget.

ETIP changed dramatically during its first three active years. After an initial surge of project implementation, the development of new projects slowed. But since later projects tended to be larger and more complicated than earlier ones, the program's budget remained relatively constant. Over time, projects also became less focused on technology and more concerned with agency efficiency, diffuse social benefits, and experimental methods. This trend continued into 1977, when a few large evaluation, regulatory reform, and economic analysis studies constituted the bulk of ETIP activities. Paralleling this shift in program activities were corresponding changes both in ETIP's formal structure and in its informal organization and culture.

FORMAL AND INFORMAL ORGANIZATION

From ETIP's earliest days, internal organizational dynamics have reflected the tenuousness of the program's future, uncertainties about the program's mission, and differing understandings of the program's strategy. In 1972 and 1973, for example, Glazer and Willenbrock were only "acting" ETIP directors. Their primary concern was getting the program administratively established—gathering a staff, formulating program plans, and releasing project funding. At this time, ETIP still viewed itself primarily as a broker between government and industry. Its major clients were expected to be private firms seeking relief from the adverse effects of government activities (such as specific waivers or regulation) or opportunities for closer government cooperation (such as participation in research consortia). ETIP's strategy was to solicit project proposals directly from industry. The program's purpose was to stimulate, facilitate, coordinate, and manage cooperative activities. The program's focus was explicitly on technological development.

This kind of program required a rather different structure than that of the later ETIP. There was no need for independent program areas that would be responsible for experimental development, since project ideas would be suggested by outside clients. Administrative functions were centralized in two deputy directors: one responsible for internal operations, the other for soliciting ideas and interacting with the public. Other program staff were expected to serve merely as contract managers and monitors, making sure that projects were being implemented as planned.

For quite some time, however, there simply were no projects to administer. The response of private industry to ETIP's solicitations was extremely poor. As a result, ETIP began refocusing its efforts on public-sector initiatives. Given private-sector indifference, this was, at least in part, a survival tactic. In part it reflected a rethinking of how a small program like ETIP could exert maximum leverage. In any case, ETIP's seven original interest areas (small inventors, procurement, waivers of regulation, and so forth) were reformulated to focus on general policy hypotheses, rather than on specific industry problems.

By early 1973 little progress had been made. The Department of Commerce had not yet released any project funds—understandably, given the instability that ETIP's staff had demonstrated. During the program's first sixteen months, ETIP not only had two acting directors, but a nearly 200 percent turnover in other personnel.

Much of the problem was caused by DoC's (and NBS's) own ambivalence toward a new program imposed by presidential mandate. DoC was unsure about the program's future and about its own commitment. ETIP was able to attract several young staffers, excited by the opportunity to work in a new, experimental program, but as time passed and nothing happened, many of these people left. Most of those who remained were not ambitious young professionals, but bureaucrats who had been "ripped" from other disbanded programs. For these individuals, ETIP was only a temporary home, a good vantage point from which to look for more permanent possibilities, but not a particularly stable base. Soon, ETIP had developed a reputation as a short-term resting place—a program that was not doing very much and that was not very long for the bureaucratic world.

In this case, the common wisdom was proved wrong. The ideas behind ETIP proved to have high-level support. By mid-1973, an ETIP Evaluation Panel had been formed at the National Academy of Sciences—both to review program activities and to serve as a distinguished group of program advisers and advocates. Soon the Department of Commerce had released funds for ETIP's initial procurement, R&D, and fabric-flammability studies. The time for a more permanent program director had come.

When Jordan Lewis became ETIP's director late in 1973, five program elements—procurement, regulation, R&D, small business, and advanced planning—had already been defined. Within this framework, Lewis quickly reorganized the staff and redefined the nature of the program's operations. The result was a new organization more clearly geared toward experimenting with public policies.

Lewis's first step after arriving at ETIP was to replace nearly all of the existing staff. Instead of recruiting cast-off civil servants, Lewis went outside the government to hire lawyers, managers, scientists, and scholars on leave from universities and private businesses. Through such term appointments, Lewis hoped to gather a dynamic staff, uninterested in government sinecures and willing to innovate in their search for innovation.

These professionals joined a program in which responsibility for project development was being decentralized. Individual staff members were expected to handle a much broader range of program activities. The two deputy directorships that had existed under Willenbrock were reduced to one, responsible for the program's bureaucratic administration. As Director, Lewis saw his major functions as policy-planning, cultivating high-level agency contacts, and developing public relations. Program area chiefs and their assistants were expected to develop, implement, manage, and evaluate their own projects. The goal was to achieve a collegial atmosphere. Weekly staff meetings provided a forum for informal guidance. Overt authority was at a minimum.

Lewis realized, however, that ETIP's future was still very insecure. Faced with pressure from both the National Bureau of Standards and the Department of Commerce, the program's first priority was to implement as many projects as possible. Lewis set funding goals for each program area during ETIP's first active fiscal year, and he pushed hard to see that they were achieved. As soon as projects were in place, Lewis quickly began to publicize their accomplishments.

By the summer of 1974, staff dissatisfaction had grown. Lewis, after all, had hired scientists and scholars whose primary aim was to gain new knowledge about public policy and innovation. Many of these staff members were uncomfortable with the constant pressure to obligate funds. They worried that ETIP's "experiments" were being developed with too little attention to scientific rigor and that they were poorly designed to add to our cumulative knowledge. Some staff members became concerned that unproven project initiatives were being trumpeted as unqualified successes. They saw the program's emphasis shifting from technological innovation toward agency trouble-shooting and the achievement of diffuse public-sector benefits. For many staff members, the time for "targets of opportunity" had ended. ETIP, they felt, should refine its priorities and become more selective in its actions.

Throughout the summer and early fall of 1974, the tempo of staff interaction increased along with the level of staff dissatisfaction. Staff meetings occurred almost daily. Hundreds of memos, notes, plans, and position papers were circulated. Finally, the disagreement erupted in a clash of personalities. By mid-fall, one group of staff members had complained directly to top NBS administrators. An organizational psychologist appeared, and began making the rounds of ETIP offices, seeking to calm unsettled emotions. By late fall, three top ETIP staffers—the economic, regulatory, and procurement chiefs—all resigned. An important phase in ETIP's life had ended.

In retrospect, Lewis's emphasis on "action" may well have been a necessary phase. Certainly, if ETIP had failed to implement a wide range of projects, the program would very likely have been disbanded. In any case, the staff replacements added during the winter of 1975 were less oriented toward science and more toward project management. Scholars and researchers were replaced by business persons and government lawyers. After a six-month lull during which controversy had displaced most project development, ETIP again began a concerted drive to implement new projects before the end of the fiscal year.

To a great extent, this effort was successful. Although the rate of project development slowed in ETIP's second active year, most of the program's budget was spent. But the turnover of personnel, and continued queries from the NAS evaluation panel, shifted the emphasis of project initiatives. Most new project development occurred in procurement and regulation; the Small Business, Research and Development, and Advanced Planning Areas became virtually defunct.

ETIP seemed a dynamic, growing, and self-assured program when my intensive field research began in the summer of 1975. The program director spoke glowingly of ETIP's potential for stimulating both private innovation and public reform. The staff presented an image of a strong commitment to change, to shaking up normally stodgy agencies, to revitalizing America's lagging technological development. The emphasis was on the program, and on the staff's commitment to the "ETIP idea." Staff members acted as if they were uninterested in bureaucratic careers, willing to take personal risks to ensure the program's progress.

Upon closer examination, the program's informal dynamics proved a bit more complicated. Tension lurked beneath the surface. Some professionals were still concerned about ETIP's overly optimistic public relations claims. Most staff members were more committed to their substantive areas—procurement, regulation, and so on—than to the program as a whole. Although there was less worry about scientific rigor, there was an increasing concern about ETIP's commitment to agency needs. A sharp division had emerged between the program area staffs and "the people behind the glass doors," the program administrators at the end of the corridor. The staff were much less interested in innovation than in solving the practical problems of the agencies with which they worked. All would be well, they thought, if ETIP would just let them work with agencies, and stop worrying about long-term technological results.

Subcultures emerged, reflecting the substantive focus of particular program areas and the professional backgrounds of staff. The primary concern in the procurement area, for example, was simply implementing more and more purchases with agency partners. Staff members hoped that this would eventually result in institutionalizing new procurement mechanisms at FSS and the VA. Although some effect on civilian innovation was desirable, experiments were not designed to rigorously test policy hypotheses. Instead, emphasis was placed on helping FSS and VA purchase better products more efficiently.

The regulatory staff also emphasized agency efficiency, but unlike the businesspersons who staffed the procurement area, they had little interest in government cost savings. Instead, these lawyers and economists identified with the missions of the agencies they served: protecting the public interest, decreasing pollution, or improving income equity. Over time, better regulation increasingly became an end in itself; technological change was only an occasional by-product.

Meanwhile, ETIP's formal structure was also changing. Under prodding from the NAS evaluation panel, ETIP became more concerned with refining the economic theory that it was supposed to be testing, and with evaluating the impact of its policy experiments. By the summer of 1975, two new program elements began coalescing. The staff economist formulated plans for an Economic Assistance Area that would not only investigate federal subsidy policies, but also study the private-sector economic incentives that all of ETIP's experiments affected. In late summer a new evaluation chief was hired and a massive Experimental Methods push was quickly organized.

By the fall of 1975, it had become clear that the ETIP staff did have a more than temporary commitment to their govern-

ment careers, and several term appointments were quietly con-
verted to civil service slots. At the same time, the staff's commitment to the "ETIP idea" was also weakening. By late fall,
the procurement chief had resigned to become Director of the
Experimental Procurement Office that he had himself helped to
create at Federal Supply. His assistant became the new procurement chief, and a procurement officer from FSS was transferred
to the ETIP staff. During the winter, the regulatory chief
resigned to join the White House regulatory reform staff. Soon,
his two assistants had resigned as well, entirely denuding the
Regulatory Area. By spring a new regulatory chief had been
added, joined shortly by an assistant, and regulatory activities
were rapidly reorganized.

By the fall of 1976, ETIP had again become very different
from what it had been only a year earlier. The previously
emerging focus on government efficiency and social benefits
was now being replaced by an ever-increasing concern with
Experimental Methods, with understanding the process of
policy change itself. The Experimental Methods chief had hired
three new assistants. Not only were a number of large evaluation studies beginning, but Experimental Methods was becoming increasingly involved in overall program analysis and project
design. The new Economic Assistance Area was growing too. A
second staff member was added and the major federal subsidy
study was inaugurated. Gears shifted, directions changed, and
the program began moving rapidly again.

By 1977, however, ETIP came under increasing scrutiny by
outside observers. Some reviews were favorable: the General
Accounting Office, for example, lauded ETIP's initiatives in life
cycle costing and recommended that new procurement procedures be disseminated throughout the bureaucracy. Other
reviews were less positive: The NAS evaluation panel was
becoming increasingly critical, and NBS and DoC administrators
were far from happy when they learned of ETIP's extensive
lobbying efforts on its own behalf. Meanwhile, ETIP's funding
remained uncertain. The program was clearly labeled "experimental," and DoC was committed to a thorough program

review, and a "go/no go" decision, by 1980. In the interim, ETIP's prospects remained clouded and its budget was uncertain from year to year. Agency partners were wary of any long-term commitments to a program that well might be on its way out.

Finally, in the spring of 1977, the new Assistant Secretary of Commerce for Science and Technology forced a resolution. He appointed a blue-ribbon panel to evaluate ETIP and make a decision about the program's future before the fiscal year's end. During the summer, the review panel met and considered a wide range of data, including my own ETIP report. On the basis of the panel's recommendation, the Assistant Secretary proposed a number of changes. As part of a more thorough reorganization, ETIP would be reconstituted as a Center for Field Methodology. It would responsible for interagency, policy change experiments focusing on substantive technological issues and would work in concert with other NBS elements. The stage was set for an entirely new phase in ETIP's evolution. My own direct involvement was at an end.

CHANGING PROGRAM GOALS

ETIP was created to investigate the relationship between public policy and innovation, to find "better ways of facilitating socially desirable technological change." The program's chosen strategy was to develop policy experiments with cooperating government agencies. Its theory focused on the effects of everyday government activities on the social and economic environment for private-sector technological decision-making. The desired results were policy change recommendations that would already be tested through agency experiments.

These were ambitious aims for a small program. They were also extremely broad aims, which offered a wide latitude for program action. Over time, ETIP's interpretation of program goals changed. As a result, the program became rather different from what its original planners had envisioned.

At the start, ETIP expected to be a troubleshooter, resolving the problems that industries face complying with government rules, cooperating in government research, or responding to government initiatives. But private industry did not want this kind of help. The 1974 Program Plan expressed ETIP's shift to a focus on public-sector initiatives. Government agencies would now be ETIP's clients. The program's primary goal had become increased knowledge—an improved understanding of the effect of government policies on the development of new technology. Yet, ETIP still saw itself as both an agent and a student of change, not just understanding innovation, but causing it. New products, and "better ways," were still the desired payoffs.

This emphasis on action—and ETIP's need to spend money—led to quick, "opportunistic" project choices. The Department of Commerce's concern for "practical" value convinced ETIP to select the most "newsworthy" projects, not necessarily the most important for understanding public policy and innovation. As a result, while many of ETIP's projects proved individually useful, they were never coherently related as a group.

But most of ETIP's agency partners were uninterested in the development of new technology. Soon ETIP's projects began deemphasizing technology goals, focusing instead on broader social benefits and public-sector efficiency. Safer drugs, better working conditions, or less costly procurement became the goal, even if no innovation were involved. And ETIP's specific concern for energy, commodities, pollution, or health care waxed or waned with the program's perception of the changing public interest.

Eventually, ETIP's goals shifted again. Most of ETIP's projects had focused on the indirect economic effects of government policies. After publication of the Gilpen report (1975), ETIP increasingly realized that the policy changes it was investigating could channel private-sector decision-making toward goals other than innovation. The Economic Assistance Area, for example, was explicitly established to investigate the multiple economic and social consequences of government subsidies.

The growing importance of ETIP's Experimental Methods Area was a natural part of this shift. ETIP's real interest was no longer in the results of policy change, but in the policy change process itself. ETIP's goal was to help other agencies improve their efficiency by serving as a methodological consultant, whatever the ultimate purpose of the policy experiments developed. Little, if any, interest in technology policy remained.

SUMMARY

ETIP's evolution can only be understood in relation to the program's position in the federal bureaucracy and the internal dynamics at both ETIP and cooperating agencies. ETIP's formal plans and rules provided only a bare outline—a rationalization, if you will—for what occurred. Within this general framework, staff members developed informal understandings about what kinds of projects could be developed. They not only sought an improved understanding of technology policy, but also personal advancement and organizational survival. Over time, ETIP changed, and its organizational culture changed too, reflecting the altered character of program staff and the shifting philosophies of program management.

ETIP's informal organization was affected by a wide range of environmental factors that had no place in the program's formal plan. The different bureaucracies with which ETIP contended had different perceptions of what the program could and should do. DoC wanted action, the development of improved products. NBS wanted rigor, the growth of scientific knowledge. Most of ETIP's agency partners cared little about either knowledge or technology. They simply wanted to do their jobs "better." If ETIP wanted agency cooperation, it had to work with individual bureaucrats seeking benefits to their personal careers. And all of these activities occurred under increasing scrutiny by the Office of Management and Budget, the National Academy of Sciences, and a number of congressional committees.

For ETIP to survive and grow, these sometimes conflicting pressures had to be reconciled. The informal understandings and procedures that developed were, in this sense, adaptive responses. At the same time, our analysis of informal program dynamics provides a more realistic basis for assessing what ETIP accomplished, what it could not or would not accomplish, and how the policy change process could be usefully improved. These are the issues that will be considered next.

NOTE

1. This section is based, in part, on ideas that were developed in Britan and Chibnik, 1980.

Chapter 7

PROGRESS, PROBLEMS, AND
POTENTIAL

Considering the obstacles faced, ETIP's record is in many ways remarkable. Among agencies noted for their conservatism, ETIP encouraged thorough reexaminations of policies and actions. In a bureaucracy renowned for minimal cooperation among agencies, ETIP opened new avenues of contact and common interest. In a government that had little concern for innovation, ETIP greatly increased policy makers' awareness of the importance of technological change. In organizations that had never "experimented," ETIP implemented wide-ranging tests of policy change. And, although ETIP's theoretical focus varied, "better ways" of stimulating innovation remained a continuing undercurrent.

ETIP's broader effects on the public sector are readily apparent. ETIP spurred numerous discussions about agency problems and heightened awareness of the technological impact of agency activities. Several of ETIP's agency partners developed their first serious interest in policy experimentation, and nearly every project received high-level agency support and involvement. By July 1976, fourteen different agencies were participating in ETIP projects, and in many cases these agencies were funding substantial portions of project costs. At the same time, nearly half of ETIP's projects involved multiple agency partners. ETIP's influence extended even further, generating a broader awareness of the importance of innovation throughout the bureaucracy and creating a far more sympathetic atmosphere toward technological change.

ETIP's specific public-sector effects are more difficult to isolate, but by 1977 some significant changes in agency attitudes and activities had occurred. At FSS, for example, ETIP accelerated the utilization of new procurement techniques and helped transcend the agency's parochial interest in purchasing costs. A special office was created to consider the broader impact of procurement policies on technological development. Still, the major outcome of ETIP's FSS project was to improve the efficiency of government procurement itself. This combined focus on public-sector efficiency and private-sector innovation was also apparent in several of ETIP's regulatory projects. Faster rate-setting, more accurate economic analysis, and more explicit standards represented improvements in the process of regulation that could also stimulate technological development. ETIP's concentration on agency goals may sometimes have resulted in too little emphasis on innovation, but lowered costs, fairer regulation, and improved economic growth were certainly desirable ends.

ETIP's effects on private industry are a bit more difficult to gauge. Even if ETIP's attempt to improve the "environment" for innovation were successful, visible responses from industry would take some time to appear. Although no substantial increase in innovation had occurred by 1977, ETIP's small-scale experiments were never intended to transform industry, but rather to gain the knowledge needed for broader policy recommendations. Unfortunately, such recommendations were never formulated. ETIP's projects were not coherently designed to test clear-cut policy change hypotheses. Indeed, the policy change process proved rather different from what ETIP had envisioned. Itself a part of the bureaucracy, ETIP faced underlying issues that it could neither escape nor resolve.

However laudable, ETIP's limited success at policy change was not always relevant to ETIP's larger purpose. The program cast its net widely. Its diverse projects addressed a range of problems that extended far beyond technological development. Despite the value of individual projects, ETIP failed in its

broader search for improved innovation policies. The reasons
are nearly as diverse as the program itself.

PROGRAM PURPOSE

ETIP's origin, history, and planning make it quite clear that
ETIP's formal mission was to investigate the relationship
between public policy and innovation. Yet technological innovation was only distantly and indirectly connected to ETIP's
everyday activities. Most of ETIP's policy experiments involved
long and complicated causal chains. There was no inevitable link
between many ETIP-initiated changes and desired technological
effects.

ETIP's actions—its choices of agency partners and experimental topics—were supposed to be guided by existing theories
about the relationships among government policies, economic
incentives, industrial decisions, and technological outcomes.
This "theory" was supposed to tell ETIP what issues were most
important and what projects were most significant. But relevant
policy theory proved remarkably weak. We really know very
little about the effect of government activities on microeconomic incentives in general, or on technological innovation
in particular. As a result, ETIP's "theoretical understandings"
usually boiled down to a few simple and untested propositions:
"Government commitments to purchase better products could
'pull' new technology into the marketplace"; "regulation
imposed barriers to technological change by increasing uncertainties and costs"; "R&D funding paid too little attention to a
product's eventual commercial sale." These are not statements
of science, but of common "wisdom"—they represent essentially political positions.

ETIP's interest in technological change defined an extremely
broad mission. ETIP realized that nearly everything that the
government did could affect the social and economic environment for innovation. In order to act effectively, ETIP desper-
ately needed to narrow its boundaries for action and to define

priorities for using its limited resources. But when the program turned to "existing theory" it found that theory lacking.

This left ETIP in a muddle. Although the program invested a large portion of its resources in policy studies that sought to clarify the theoretical basis for policy experiments, such a passive analytical role was not what had originally been envisioned. Moreover, an unstable and politically sensitive program like ETIP was not a particularly suitable sponsor for basic research into a poorly charted area. Contractor findings simply began to reflect the biases that ETIP already held.

In a few cases, ETIP solved the problem of inadequate theory by focusing on policies that directly affected innovation. As a result, the program's clearest technological relevance can be found in its work with inventors, research consortia, and R&D funding agencies. But ETIP's major concern remained the everyday government practices that altered the broader social and economic environment in which innovation occurred.

The lack of precise theoretical guidelines most often resulted in what could be called an "opportunistic" project selection strategy. Since experiments required agency cooperation anyway, ETIP decided to concentrate on problems that agencies themselves perceived as important. Given the inadequacy of existing theory, nearly any effort could eventually be rationalized as relevant to innovation. As a result, ETIP's projects developed piecemeal, without any consistent technological focus.

The problem was compounded by the fact that many of the policy changes tested by ETIP had no necessary or immediate link to industrial innovation. ETIP was well aware that its attempt to manipulate microeconomic incentives could have been aimed at a variety of civilian-sector results. Over time, the program increasingly emphasized the diffuse social benefits that its policy change experiments could achieve. Unfortunately, our understanding of the relationship among government policies, economic incentives, and social benefits is no better than our understanding of public policy and innovation. ETIP found even fewer theoretical guidelines for the more general policy change role that it sometimes pursued.

The problems with ETIP's technology focus were basic and difficult to solve. ETIP's search for "better ways" was guided by very general theoretical principles. The range of potentially relevant policy experiments was enormous. ETIP solved the problem through an opportunistic project selection strategy that shifted program goals toward issues of public-sector efficiency and policy change methodology. ETIP became a kind of agency troubleshooter, but the rhetoric of "innovation" remained.

PROGRAM STRATEGY

The problem of program purpose was further complicated by related questions about program strategy: How should ETIP proceed? What specific results should be gained from ETIP's efforts? What would be the appropriate mixture of research and action? These questions might seem superfluous, since the 1974 Program Plan clearly designated ETIP's policy experimentation strategy. But the Program Plan also noted that the primary measure of ETIP's success would be knowledge gained, and more than half of the projects that ETIP developed were passive policy studies.

Certainly, there was ambiguity. On the one hand, ETIP saw itself as a seeker of knowledge, learning about the relationship between public policy and innovation. But at the same time, ETIP also saw itself as a change agent, altering agency behavior and stimulating the development of new technology for the civilian marketplace. Sometimes the roles conflicted. ETIP often felt that more research was needed to provide a foundation for action but, at the same time, was pressured to demonstrate that its actions could stimulate technological development.

In retrospect, ETIP's "knowledge-seeker" and "change-agent" roles were essential complements. If ETIP truly sought an improved understanding of the effects of policy change, the best way to learn was through experience. Government procedures would have to be altered, and worthwhile changes would most likely be institutionalized. But to be an effective change agent, ETIP had to be as concerned with the scientific rigor of its projects as with their political acceptability.

The complementarity of ETIP's knowledge-seeker and change-agent roles should have had important implications for program action. First of all, it meant that the policy changes that ETIP initiated did not always have to be successful. To a scientist, the absence of effects is just as important as the presence; if results were certain, there would be no reason to conduct policy experiments in the first place.

However, this complementarity of roles did not indicate that ETIP needed such a large number of analytical studies, and the utility of many of these studies can be seriously questioned. The policies that ETIP investigated were, in essence, theories about the effects of government actions. Sometimes such policy "theories" can be fairly well grounded. The government, for example, is fairly certain that food stamps help poor people obtain more nutritious meals. But the validity of most policy theories is less clear: Does the death penalty really deter crime? Does welfare destroy the work ethic? Is solar power the solution to America's energy shortage? These questions can be researched, but when previously developed theory is weak and when issues are politically contentious, such research is often suspect. This was, of course, exactly ETIP's situation. Not only was technology policy poorly understood, but ETIP was focusing on complex, indirect relationships. ETIP's contractors frequently "discovered" precise policy solutions, but these results seem to have stemmed less from insight and more from the nature of consultancy research itself.

Unlike academic studies, contracted consultancy research usually involves short deadlines and tight schedules, sharply limiting the depth to which problems can be investigated. Most agencies naturally seek out contractors with compatible backgrounds and viewpoints. When theory is weak, data are soft, and time is limited, the findings of these researchers are as much interpretation as fact. It is not surprising that consultancy research so often mirrors the perspectives of its agency sponsors. The government is littered with thousands of consultant studies that provide little more than politically useful documentation for positions and biases already held.

One of the most important aspects of ETIP's policy experimentation strategy was that it avoided many of the problems of such consultancy research. Despite their long chains of causality, ETIP's experimental hypotheses could at least in principle be disproved. When issues are complex and theories ill-defined, consultancy studies can usually add little to our understanding. Policy experimentation, on the other hand, is certainly a "strategy" through which forces of change and sources of knowledge can be usefully combined.

AGENCY COOPERATION

ETIP's policy experimentation strategy required the cooperation of other government agencies. ETIP needed to develop agency contacts, to identify areas of agency concern, to generate trust, and to formulate joint projects meeting mutual needs. Negotiating agency relationships was a delicate process, but one at which ETIP proved effective. Many of the program's agency partners enthusiastically supported the changes that ETIP initiated.

There were limits, however, to this spirit of cooperation, which placed important restrictions on the kinds of projects that ETIP could implement. No agency would invest its time or resources in projects which were antithetical, or even merely irrelevant, to its interests. Agencies wanted to see direct advantages—eliminated problems, increased efficiency, or enhanced policy effectiveness—before they would join in an ETIP project. As a result, there were many potentially relevant policy changes in which agencies had little interest.

ETIP's own lack of priorities and boundaries made the identification of technologically relevant areas of cooperation more difficult. ETIP lacked guidelines for deciding when an agency's willingness to cooperate would result in a project that fulfilled the program's own interests. ETIP, of course, was also under strong external pressure to develop agency ties and implement projects. Thus, ETIP faced a strong temptation to continue project development whenever agency cooperation was likely. Clearer selection criteria might have made it easier for ETIP to avoid projects that were irrelevant to program goals. But from ETIP's perspective, nearly any feasible project was worth doing.

PROGRAM CHANGE

Early in my research, one ETIP staff member pointedly told me that nothing at ETIP was as constant as change. At the time, he was referring to the program's initial years, to the rapid shifts in policy and leadership as the program groped for its place in the bureaucracy. Yet even after a formal program plan was written, ETIP continued to change rapidly. New procedures, new projects, new policies, new goals—everything was continually transformed as ETIP searched for opportunities, influence, power, and survival. Underlying these shifts, and ETIP's remarkable inconsistency, has been a continuing problem with staff departure.

Between 1972 and 1974 ETIP had three directors and a nearly complete turnover of staff; between 1974 and 1976 most of this staff was replaced again; by 1977 a third wave of turnovers was occurring—replacements for the replacements of the replacements. No program can develop well-integrated plans with a basic structure that is so unstable. Each time that new staff members had to be enculturated, agency relationships became strained, project development became stalled, and advanced planning was inhibited. ETIP's organizational culture became heavily weighted toward the personal interests of whatever staff members were on board.

As a result, the program became dominated by its informal organization (see Britan and Cohen, 1980a). Day-to-day program policy was increasingly determined by the politics of program staff. Program activities began to closely reflect the changing personal interests, experiences, and backgrounds of available personnel. When ETIP was composed primarily of scientists and engineers, it focused on the rigorous testing of policy hypotheses. When it was composed of lawyers and businesspersons, it focused on government efficiency and social benefits. When it was composed of evaluators, it focused on experimental methodology.

Periodically, ETIP's director would reassert himself and decide that a change in program direction was indicated. One group of staff members would depart and a new group would appear. The result was an organizational culture in which personal self-interest became far more important than program loyalty. No one expected ETIP to be around for very long, and in any case the program was sure to change in unpredictable ways. But ETIP was also a highly visible program, where an ambitious person could make a mark before moving on.

For ETIP, it was a vicious circle. A loosely defined program mandate and a weak theoretical base produced changing priorities, staff disagreements, and staff departures. At the same time, the high rate of staff turnover made implementing a consistent plan of action nearly impossible. The situation was further exacerbated by continuing uncertainties about the program's future and by an organizational climate in which clashes of personality came to the fore. The result was a program which in many ways never even tried to achieve its long-term goals.

SUMMARY

ETIP was an important program. It demonstrated that bureaucratic agencies could experiment with new policies, that government efficiency could be improved, and that federal planning could be fine-tuned. It also called attention to the crucial role that innovation plays in ensuring our nation's economic welfare.

Yet, despite these accomplishments, ETIP achieved few substantive results. It was never able to stimulate technological development significantly; it never clarified the relationship between public policy and innovation; it was never a major force for bureaucratic reform. ETIP was spread too thin, it moved too fast, and it changed too often. The program could not successfully apply all of its many interesting ideas.

ETIP was a program of limited resources, but because it lacked clearly defined boundaries, it was faced with an extremely broad range of possible activities. The problem was exacerbated by ETIP's continuing uncertainty about its proper role, and its continuing problems in program administration.

ETIP was initiated as an experiment. It combined an innovative strategy with weak theory to create an eclectic program that was unable to improve American innovation policy substantially. Viewed as an experiment, however, ETIP does provide us with much useful knowledge about the process of policy change itself. It is here that the program's broader significance lies.

Chapter 8

ETIP'S BROADER SIGNIFICANCE

Bureaucracies often resist change, but not because of any intrinsic organizational inertia. ETIP's projects demonstrated that a source of policy change could be introduced without drastically altering the structure of government. The program's founders hoped that a small organization with exciting new ideas could significantly affect the operation of federal agencies. Our research has shown that this hope was both partially realized and, at the same time, overly optimistic.

At the very least, ETIP's experience showed that many government agencies were willing to experiment with new policies. These bureaucracies did not, however, operate in a vacuum, but were strongly affected by the social, political, and economic setting within which they existed. Even when the benefits of changes were demonstrated, this did not mean that changes would be implemented or that larger policies would be altered. Just the same, the lack of adequate proof did not necessarily mean that a policy would be abandoned. The process of policy changes was simply not completely "rational." ETIP's relationship to American innovation policy is a case in point.

ETIP'S EPILOGUE: "SUCCESS" OUT OF "FAILURE"

Government programs never die, but are reborn with different names. After being reviewed by the Assistant Secretary of Commerce in 1977, ETIP was slated to become the experimental methods coordinator for a reorganized industrial innovation task force at the National Bureau of Standards. But the

Office of Management and Budget never approved the Bureau's intended restructuring and for the next three years ETIP remained in a curious limbo. By the end of 1977, Lewis had resigned as ETIP's director and was replaced "temporarily" by his former deputy. Funding for existing projects was continued, but except for occasional evaluations, few new projects were started. By 1980, it was being suggested that ETIP's remnants be transferred to the Assistant Secretary's office to serve as a research and experimental methods resource.

Although a number of individual ETIP projects attracted considerable interest, by 1980 it was clear that the program as a whole had failed to achieve its larger goals. ETIP's studies and experiments had not gained significant new knowledge that could improve American innovation policy. At best, the program had provided some piecemeal examples. It never demonstrated that government procurement could pull new technology into the marketplace; that more accurate regulation could stimulate new product development; that more refined R&D funding could improve the odds of commercial success. On the contrary, the results of several ETIP projects cast serious doubt on basic program hypotheses.

Just the same, American innovation policy was transformed during the decade of the 1970s. Despite ETIP's failures, many of ETIP's ideas have now been accepted as policy gospel. According to current political wisdom, government purchasing can stimulate technological development, federal regulation does impose unnecessary barriers to innovation, and federal subsidies can encourage private-sector investment. ETIP's commitment to increasing productivity through innovation has become part of the core of the "new" supply-side economics that is sweeping fashionable circles in Washington and academia.

A serious analysis of the political process that lies behind this major policy shift is beyond the scope of this book. Such an analysis would have to consider wide-ranging issues of changing international trade, domestic economics, national politics, and scholarly debate. In principle, ETIP was created to help develop a rigorous experimental basis for these new policy theories. In fact, the program itself was a part of the political process of policy change.

ETIP was established because some of this country's senior policy makers saw America approaching an economic crisis. Productivity and trade were lagging. One major cause was the country's falling rate of innovation. Big-technology policies had already failed. A new solution was sought through industrial incentive policies that would free the "free market" from excessive government interference. And what proved congenial to one Republican administration became, with minor modifications, the central political wisdom of the 1980s.

Some participant or researcher may eventually unravel the political process through which this new innovation policy emerged. ETIP, certainly, was not so much the cause of this shift as it was a by-product. ETIP was created to test new policies, but once in existence the program simply became another factor in the political equation. Its projects, its studies, its publicity, its lobbying—all affected the policy debate. ETIP, of course, played a minor role, but one in which the appearance of ETIP's success was much more important than the facts of specific failures. In any case, most of the policy changes that ETIP proposed never received anything like a rigorous assessment.

POLICY EXPERIMENTS AND POLICY CHANGE

What, then, can ETIP teach us about the process of policy change and the potential of policy experiments as mechanisms of policy improvement? Government bureaucracies may not be entirely rational, but our research has shown that agencies often do seek to improve their efficiency and effectiveness. To the extent that this is true, experimentation can play an important role in the policy change process.

ETIP's experience also demonstrated some of the limits of bureaucratic rationality. ETIP's formal mission was to test new ways of stimulating industrial innovation. The program presented a public image of commitment to change, experimentation, innovation, and reform, but the private reality was more pedestrian. ETIP and its staff were seeking to survive and prosper in an environment that buffeted them with constantly conflicting pressures. The bottom line was not formulating better innovation policies, but obligating money, implementing projects, satisfying agencies, and developing a program constituency. Despite ETIP's public statements about encouraging technological development, informal understandings increasingly emphasized ETIP's role in solving agency-perceived problems. Over time, the result was a shift in program goals toward social benefits, government efficiency, and methodological consulting.

ETIP's agency partners faced similar pressures. Whatever their formal mission—purchasing products, promoting railroads, or protecting the public interest—the first and foremost concern of every agency was bureaucratic survival. Here too, substance was often less important than appearance. In order to prosper, agencies had to demonstrate that they were filling important needs and that they were responding to political demands. Program effectiveness—improved public policies—were only important within this limited context. No agency worried about efficiency or effectiveness unless this was also in that agency's political interest.

At the same time, the development of ETIP's policy experiments did involve a personal dynamic. The professional background of some agency staff made them more sympathetic to ETIP's ideas. Personal careers could sometimes be advanced through participation in ETIP initiatives. But ETIP staff members had personal goals too, and their careers often became identified with agency concerns. Witness, for example, the number of professionals who left ETIP to work for agencies that had originally been experiment partners.

What all of this means is that the potential for *cooperative* policy experiments is limited. A small, unstable program like ETIP, with a poorly defined policy mandate, could provide little more than agency troubleshooting. It offered funding, expertise, and sponsorship for projects that were essentially agency affairs. Even if ETIP had had a solider base and a firmer grasp of its mission, the best that could have been accomplished would have been to ensure that projects represented truly mutual interests.

Would policy experiments prove more useful in other program settings? The answer seems to be both "yes" and "no." Few agencies have any abstract interest in better policies, but many would like to improve their own policy implementation. It is here that the greatest potential for policy experiments lies.

The issue may become clearer if we consider precisely what we mean by "policy change." Policies involve two elements. First, they represent value judgments about appropriate goals— anything from increased racial integration to production of more fuel-efficient automobiles. Second, they represent theories about how these goals can be achieved—through school busing to promote integration or regulations to prohibit "gas guzzlers."

Government agencies cannot make "rational" decisions about the kinds of ends that should be pursued. These are determined through political processes, in the largest sense. Even when agencies must interpret or redefine policy goals, this does not result from scientific research so much as from bureaucratic pressure, professional culture, or constituency interests.

In most cases, this is also true of policy theories, ideas about how policy goals can be achieved. Although such theories may, in principle, be testable, decisions about policy implementation are more often based on ideology than science (see, for example, Rule, 1979). Is busing or local school excellence the way to improve ghetto education? Is regulation or taxation the way to achieve fuel efficiency? Witness the current debate about controlling the economy, and remember that the theoretical underpinnings of most social programs are far weaker.

In my view, many social scientists have overrated the value of policy experimentation as a basis for policy improvement (e.g., Reiken et al., 1974). Experiments, after all, are simply rational methods for logical (and statistical) inference. They work best when well-defined theories provide a clear basis for drawing conclusions from controlled comparisons. But our theories of

social change are not that strong. Our understanding of the
relationships between policy causes and human effects encompasses too many sources of error. Many of our "policies" are
directed at multiple, and not necessarily compatible, ends.
Experimentation may sound scientific, but the creation of more
effective public policies remains an essentially political art.

This does not mean that policy experiments are useless, but
that their utility lies less in improved policy-making than in
improved policy administration. ETIP's experience indicates
that agencies are interested in the latter, and thus are often
willing to experiment more narrowly with alternative methods
for achieving politically defined goals. FSS does want to purchase products more cost-effectively; FDA wants the most
efficient postmarketing surveillance system; FPC wants public
utilities to conduct more accurate economic analyses. Final
goals or basic theories are not at issue; what is, is simply how
given policies can most effectively be implemented. And it is in
the study of this policy implementation that organizational
ethnography has a critical role to play.

THE FUTURE OF ORGANIZATIONAL ETHNOGRAPHY

"Ethnography" today has become something of a Washington buzzword. Ethnographers, someone discovered, gain unexpected insights, and suddenly dozens of federal studies are
including an "ethnographic" component. Unfortunately, much
of this ethnography amounts to little more than a minimum of
firsthand observation by untrained researchers during a few site
visits.

Even when properly conducted, ethnography cannot provide
a panacea. It is a set of techniques—heavily biased toward
participant observation—for gaining in-depth, multidimensional
understandings of social contexts. It provides a means of enter-
ing the world of the "native," and of relating this world to the
categories of the scientific observer.

In the realm of policy analysis and evaluation, ethnography
rarely provides unequivocal judgments about program effectiveness. It cannot, like experimental tests, imply unequivocal

causes and effects. Then again, few programs have the clear goals, well-defined theories, and specific treatments that make experimental assessments useful and valid (see, for example, Britan 1978a, 1978b). The issue in most cases is not the validity of program theory, but the nature and meaning of program implementation. This is precisely what an ethnography can most effectively reveal.

This ethnography of the Experimental Technology Incentives Program examined both the formal and informal realities of program implementation. It looked at what ETIP said, what it did, how it operated, how it changed, and why it departed from its initial plans. It viewed ETIP's organization as a living social system, composed of conscious members adapting to a constantly changing environment. It not only considered ETIP's formal plans, but also the informal understandings and relationships that reflected practical pressures of bureaucratic life and the backgrounds, biases, and wishes of individual staff members. It sought to describe ETIP as it was, not as some participants would have liked it to be.

ETIP's evolution resulted from a rather complicated combination of organizational, political, and environmental factors. It would be inaccurate to interpret the findings simply as an indication that it was "the nature of the bureaucracy" that prevented ETIP from stimulating meaningful change. ETIP did see itself as a catalyst for policy improvement, but it was a small program that could have little effect so long as its own objectives remained unfocused. This is the reason that my original report strongly recommended that ETIP return to a clearer focus on technology—a step that could increase the program's ability to significantly affect public policy.

Although it is true that bureaucracies often resist change, explaining this in terms of the "essential inertia of bureaucracy" is, at best, a gross oversimplification. Bureaucracies do not operate in a vacuum. They are affected by the personal and professional characteristics (the subcultural backgrounds) of their members and by the political, social, and economic context of bureaucratic culture itself. This context can at times retard innovation and reinforce bureaucratic "stodginess," but at other times it can also serve as a stimulus for change.

These statements are not meant as truisms, but rather as arguments to spend less time studying policy theory and more time studying policy *implementation*. Much of this research should involve in-depth ethnography that can identify the informal social and cultural processes through which bureaucrats and bureaucracies adapt. This study has taken a first step. But organizational ethnography faces a challenging future if it is to help meet the human needs of our increasingly bureaucratic world.

APPENDIX A

ETIP PROJECTS BY NUMBER

1. Power Lawn Mower Procurement Experiment
2. Room Air Conditioner Procurement Experiment
3. Frostless Refrigerator Procurement Experiment
4. Home Water Heater Procurement Experiment
5. Kitchen Range Procurement Experiment
6. Agency-Initiated Design of Procurement Experiments
7. Fiber, Textile, and Apparel Flammability Research Institute
8. Dynamics of Regulatory Effects of Innovation
9. Imperfections in Capital Markets.
10. Analysis of Reasons for Nonacquisition of Independent Inventions by Corporations and Patent Broker/Developers
11. Analysis of Federal Demonstration Projects
12. Commercial Potential of Federal Invention Disclosures Rejected for Patent Filing
13. Diffusion of University Research Output
14. Guidelines for Industrial R&D Aggregation
15. Enhancing the General Welfare of U.S. Industry
16. Development of Models for Selecting Technology-Stimulating Policy Tools
17. Federal Contingency Planning for Anticipated Technological Crisis
18. Development of Institutional Planning Framework for Cooperative Public-Private Sector Civilian R&D
19. Federal Funding of Civilian R&D
20. Creation of National Product Marketing Service
21. Impact of the Regulatory Process on Industrial Innovation
22. Use of Regulatory Authority to Stimulate Nonmandated Technological Change
23. Impact of the Institutional Organization of Government Regulation on Technological Development and Use

24. Public Safety Equipment Development
25. Analysis of Barriers to Technological Change for ETIP Procurement Experiments
26. Mandated Technological Change
27. Development of Procedures for Evaluating Technology-Based Firms for SBA Funding
28. Assisting Small Firms Required by Regulation to Undergo Technological Change
29. Conference on Federal/Industrial Partnership in New Product Development
30. Intergovernmental Conference on Public Civilian Technology Policy
31. Refrigerated Rail Transport Experiment
32. Connecticut Product Development Corporation
33. An Examination of the Interrelationship Between the R&D Funding Activity and Regulatory Activity of EPA
34. Providing Incentives for Large Users of Electrical Energy to Use It More Efficiently
35. Life Cycle Costing Applied to the Procurement Process
36. LCC Guide for Evaluating Building Design Alternatives
37. Increasing Health-Care Productivity Through an Improved Selection of Technologies
38. Experiments in the Use of Performance Specifications to Stimulate Desirable Technological Change in Health-Care Equipment
39. Development of Guidelines for the Use of Performance vs. Design Specifications in Procurement
40. Design of Three Procurement Experiments
41. Design of Additional Procurement Experiments
42. Investigation of Procurement Opportunities
43. Government Market Research for Procurement Guidance
44. Design of Regulatory Experiments for Narrow-Scope Agencies
45. Design of Regulatory Experiments for Broad-Scope Agencies
46. Competency Evaluation of Small R&D Firms
47. Accelerating the Licensing of Nuclear Power Reactors
48. Regulating Toxic Substances
49. Regulating the Irradiation of Foods
50. Regulation of Renewable Resources
51. Design of Prototype Regulations for State PUCs for Energy Conservation
52. Regulating New Pharmaceuticals

53. Government/Industry Joint Venture in R&D
54. Accelerating the Use of Solar Energy Research
55. Technology Impact Statements
56. Geothermal Energy Technology Delivery System
57. Intersectoral Transfer of a Building Technology by a Major User
58. Automobile Tires
59. ADP Ribbon Procurement Experiment
60. Public Market Aggregation as an Incentive for Technological Change
61. Biomedical Monitoring Systems (BMS) Procurement Experiment
62. Blood Tubes Procurement Experiment
63. Internally Oriented Life Cycle Costing (LCC) Program for Federal Purchasing
64. Value Incentive Contracting Program for Federal Purchasing
65. Utilizing University Research in Transportation
66. Technical Evaluation
67. Modular Integrated Utility System
68. Institutional Evaluation
69. The Cooperative Agreement as a Mechanism for Technology Utilization
70. Payment of Costs Incurred by the Federal Supply Service in Providing Background Information and Conducting Preliminary Studies on Potential ETIP Projects
71. Cleaning Agent Procurement Experiment
72. Technical Assistance to the Procurement Policy Area of ETIP
73. Oscilloscopes
74. Furniture
75. Systematizing Local Procurement as the Preface to Technological Change
76. Experiments in Computer Application to Regulatory Agencies
77. Symposium in Assistance to Small Technology-Based Firms
78. Data Collection, Summarization, and Interpretation for ETIP Project with Connecticut Product Development Corporation
79. Survey of Five-Year Results of Innovation Loan Program
80. Systematizing the Design, Development, and Use of Incentives in the Procurement of Medical Equipment and Supplies
81. Design of Federal Procurement Experiments for Improved Health-Care Delivery
82. Office Copiers
83. Information Management in Procurement

84. Regulation, Competition, and Innovation
85. Using Technology to Increase the Information and Decrease the Time for Regulatory Process
86. Experiment in Contractor Selection
87. Management of Federal Civilian Research and Development Programs
88. Experiment in Clinical Testing of Drug Efficiency
89. The Connecticut Experiment
90. Evaluation of Federal Supply Service Procurement Experiments
91. Evaluating State and Local Procurements
92. [not used]
93. Federal Financial Assistance and Technological Change
94. Evaluation of ETIP
95. Evaluation of ETIP Project to Accelerate Nuclear Standards
96. Real-Time Case History of ETIP Project 67 (MIUS)
97. Evaluation of an Interorganizational Consortium for Research and Development Management
98. Improving the Standards-Setting Process
99. Expanded Nuclear Standards Project
100. Regulation of Competition
101. Antitrust Boundary Project
102. Regulatory Degree Project
103. Evaluate Standards Projects
104. Evaluate Economic Regulation
105. Evaluating Certification Projects
106. Confirming Procurements (FSS)
107. Design of Procurment Experiments
108. Monitoring Assistance
109. Federal Procurement of Health-Related Goods (evaluation)
110. Space Procurement (evaluation)
111. Market Planning Project
112. R&D Projects (evaluation)
113. Test Loan Evaluation Procedure
114. Test Small Business Regulatory Compliance Procedures
115. Exploratory Analysis
116. Case Studies in Procurement
117. The Implementation of Life Cycle Costing at Federal Supply Service—An Evaluation Plan for the Agency Effects of the Implementation
118. Window Air Conditioners—Second cycle

119. Evaluate LCC Seminars
120. Commercial and Technological Impact of the Procurement Experiments
121. The Agency and Limited Commercial Effects of the ETIP Procurement Experiments
122. The Agency Effects of Policy Changes Implemented on the Basis of ETIP Procurement Experiments
123. Case Studies in Procurement—Value Incentive Clause
124. Technical Assistance to Procurement Program Area of ETIP
125. Flammable Fabrics Symposium
126. An Expanded Program for the Dissemination of Results from a Team Project for the Development of Flame-Resistant Polyester/Cotton Fabrics
127. Workshops on Technology and the Law
128. Campus-Community Integrated Utility System
129. Procurement of Fire-Retardant Paint
130. Citizens' Conference on State Legislatures
131. Warranty
132. Refinement and Dissemination of Policy Issues for Contingency Planning for Anticipated Crises in Commodity Supplies
133. National Conference of State Legislatures
134. Evaluation of Consortium Results
135. Energy Volume Expansion
136. Small Business (design of analysis)
137. Technical Information Assistance to Procurement

APPENDIX B

ONGOING AND COMPLETED PROJECTS

Project Number	Project Type	Project Status	Funding (dollars)	Lead Agency	Contract Recipient	Date of Transfer or Award
Procurement						
1	experiment	active	30,000	FSS	Fedders, GE	FY 74
2	experiment	active	30,000	FSS	Philco-Ford,	FY 74
3	experiment	active	30,000	FSS	GE, Hotpoint	FY 74
4	experiment	active	30,000	FSS	A. O. Smith	FY 74
5	experiment	active	36,000	FSS	Sunray, Roper	FY 74
29	other	completed	self-supporting	ETIP	—	N.A.
36	experiment	active	175,000	FSS	Mariscal	FY 74
38	exp. design	completed	123,000	ETIP	Ross Hofmann Associates	FY 74
40	exp. design	completed	35,000	ETIP	Booz-Allen, Hamilton, Inc.	FY 74
41	exp. design	active	95,000	ETIP	Booz-Allen, Hamilton, Inc.	FY 74
42	experiment	active	400,000	FSS	ORSA	FY 74
59	experiment	active	19,000	FSS	—	FY 74

No.	Type	Status	Program	Amount	Contractor	FY
60	experiment	active	ETIP	278,000	CSG-NASPO	FY 75
63	other	active	FSS	200,000	Logistics Management Inst.	FY 74
64	other	active	FSS	66,000	Stanford Research Inst.	FY 74
70	other	active	FSS	50,000	–	FY 74
72	other	completed	ETIP	49,000	Charles Travis	FY 75
74	experiment	active	FSS	110,000	Purdue University	FY 76
75	experiment	active	ETIP	314,000	CSG-NIGP	FY 75
80	other	active	VA	450,000	Ross Hofmann Associates	FY 75
116	general study	active	ETIP	10,000	Logistics Management Inst.	FY 76
118	evaluation	completed	FSS	10,000	Logistics Management Inst.	FY 76
119	evaluation	active	ETIP	20,000	Tash & Zamoff	FY 76
120	evaluation	active	ETIP	899,000	Stanford Research Institute	FY 76
121	evaluation	active	ETIP	889,000	Research Triangle Institute	FY 76
123	general study	active	ETIP	10,000	Kemple, Rossman Associates	FY 76
124	other	active	ETIP	48,000	Charles Travis	FY 76
129	experiment	developing	FSS	50,000	–	FY 77
130	general study	completed	ETIP	10,000	–	FY 76
131	experiment	developing	FSS	50,000	–	FY 77
137	other	active	ETIP	10,000	M. L. Schropp	FY 76

Regulation

No.	Type	Status	Program	Amount	Contractor	FY
8	general study	active	ETIP	169,000	Charleswater Associates	FY 75
31	experiment	active	FRA	150,000	Manalytics, Inc.	FY 74

Project Number	Project Type	Project Status	Funding (dollars)	Lead Agency	Contract Recipient	Date of Transfer Or Award
44	exp. design	completed	115,000	ETIP	Gellman Research Associates	FY 74
45	exp. design	completed	124,000	ETIP	Public Interest Economics Center	FY 74
47	experiment	completed	100,000	AEC	Battelle Northwest	FY 74
48	general study	active	250,000	EPA	Arthur D. Little Co.	FY 74
76	experiment	active	363,000	FPC	Temple, Barker & Sloan	FY 75
85	experiment	active	200,000	OSHA	—	FY 75
88	experiment	active	1,100,000	FDA	—	FY 76
95	evaluation	active	40,000	ETIP	ANSI	FY 75
127	other	active	95,000	ABA	ABA	FY 76
R & D						
7	other	completed	475,000	ETIP	Clemson University	FY 74
11	general study	completed	324,000	ETIP	RAND	FY 74
13	experiment	active	99,400	NSF	Research Corporation	FY 74
19	general study	completed	296,000	ETIP	Arthur D. Little Co.	FY 74
67	experiment	active	220,000	HEW	Geiringer Associates, Reynolds, Smith & Hills	FY 75
96	evaluation	active	34,000	ETIP	Systems Planning Corporation	FY 76
97	evaluation	active	9,000	ETIP	RAND	FY 76

125	other	active	10,000	ETIP	Clemson University	FY 76
126	other	active	43,000	ETIP	Clemson University	FY 76
134	evaluation	active	10,000	ETIP	RAND	FY 76

Small Business

9	general study	completed	296,000	ETIP	Charles River Associates	FY 74
28	general study	completed	200,000	SBA	Charleswater Associates	FY 74
32	experiment	active	300,000	ETIP	CPDC	FY 74
46	general study	active	375,000	SBA	Innovative Systems Research	FY 74
77	other	completed	10,000	ETIP	Amer. Assn. of Small R&D Companies	FY 75
78	evaluation	active	159,000	ETIP	Charleswater Associates	FY 75
79	general study	completed	45,000	ETIP	Moshman Associates	FY 75
89	evaluation	completed	3,000	ETIP	K. E. Willis	FY 76

Economic Assistance

17	general study	completed	297,000	ETIP	Charles River Associates	FY 74
93	general study	active	475,000	ETIP	Charles River Associates	FY 76
132	other	active	40,000	ETIP	Charles River Associates	FY 76
135	general study	developing	8,500	ETIP	Charles River Associates	FY 77
136	evaluation	developing	10,000	ETIP	G. W. Barth & others	FY 77

APPENDIX C

ETIP PROJECTS BY PROGRAM AREA

PROCUREMENT

1. Power Lawn Mower Procurement Experiment
2. Room Air Conditioner Procurement Experiment
3. Frostless Refrigerator Procurement Experiment
4. Home Water Heater Procurement Experiment
5. Kitchen Range Procurement Experiment
29. Conference on Federal/Industrial Partnership in New Product Development
36. LCC Guide for Evaluating Building Design Alternatives (new title: Design and Use of LCC Models for the Planning and Acquisition of Federal Space)
38. Experiments in the Use of Performance Specifications to Stimulate Desirable Technological Change in Health-Care Equipment
40. Design of Three Procurement Experiments
41. Design of Additional Procurement Experiments
42. Investigation of Procurement Opportunities
59. ADP Ribbon Procurement
60. Public Market Aggregation as an Incentive for Technological Change
63. Internally Oriented Life Cycle Costing (LCC) Program for Federal Purchasing
64. Value Incentive Contracting Program for Federal Purchasing
70. Payment of Costs Incurred by the Federal Supply Service in Providing Background Information and Conducting Preliminary Studies on Potential ETIP Projects
72. Technical Assistance to the Procurement Policy Area of ETIP

AUTHOR'S NOTE: Asterisks indicate inactive projects.

74. Furniture
75. Systematizing Local Procurement as the Preface to Technological Change
80. Systematizing the Design, Development, and Use of Incentives in the Procurement of Medical Equipment and Supplies
116. Case Studies in Procurement
118. Window Air Conditioners—Second Cycle
119. Evaluate LCC Seminars
120. Commercial and Technological Impact of Procurement Experiments
121. Agency and Limited Commercial Effects of ETIP Procurement Experiments
123. Case Studies in Procurement—Value Incentive Clause
124. Technical Assistance to the Procurement Program Area
129. Procurement of Fire-Retardant Paint
130. Citizens' Conference on State Legislatures
131. Warranty
137. Technical Information Assistance to Procurement
6. Agency-Initiated Design of Procurement Experiments*
25. Analysis of Barriers to Technological Change for ETIP Procurement Experiments*
35. Life Cycle Costing Applied to the Procurement Process*
37. Increasing Health-Care Productivity through an Improved Selection of Technologies*
39. Development of Guidelines for the Use of Performance vs. Design Specifications in Procurement*
43. Government Market Research for Procurement Guidance*
58. Automobile Tires*
61. Biomedical Monitoring Systems (BMS) Procurement Experiment*
62. Blood Tubes Procurement Experiment*
71. Cleaning Agent Procurement Experiment*
73. Oscilloscopes*
81. Design of Federal Procurement Experiments for Improved Health-Care Delivery*
82. Office Copiers*
83. Information Management in Procurement*
90. Evaluation of FSS Procurement Experiments*
91. Evaluating State and Local Procurements*
106. Confirming Procurements*

REGULATION

52. Regulating New Pharmaceuticals*
55. Technology Impact Statements*
84. Regulation, Competition, and Innovation*
98. Improving the Standards-Setting Process*
99. Expanded Nuclear Standards Project*
100. Regulation of Competition*
101. Antitrust Boundary Project*
102. Regulatory Degree Project*
103. Evaluate Standards Project*
104. Evaluate Economic Regulation*
105. Evaluating Certification Projects*

RESEARCH AND DEVELOPMENT

7.   Fiber, Textile, and Apparel Flammability Research Institute
11. Analysis of Federal Demonstration Projects
13. Diffusion of University Research Output
19. Federal Funding of Civilian R&D
67. Modular Integrated Utility System
96. Real-Time Case History of ETIP Project 67 (MIUS)
97. Evaluation of an Interorganizational Consortium for Research and Development Management
125. Flammable Fabrics Symposium
126. An Expanded Program for the Dissemination of Results from a Team Project for the Development of Flame-Resistant Polyester/Cotton Fabrics
134. Evaluation of Consortium Results
12. Commercial Potential of Federal Invention Disclosures Rejected for Patent Filing*
14. Guidelines for Industrial R&D Aggregation*
15. Enhancing the General Welfare of U.S. Industry*
16. Development of Models for Selecting Technology-Stimulating Policy Tools*
18. Development of Institutional Planning Framework for Cooperative Public-Private Sector Civilian R&D*
24. Public Safety Equipment Development*
30. Intergovernmental Conference on Public Civilian Technology Policy*
53. Government/Industry Joint Venture in R&D*

54. Accelerating the Use of Solar Energy Research*
56. Geothermal Energy Technology Delivery System*
57. Intersectoral Transfer of a Building Technology by a Major User*
65. Utilizing University Research in Transportation*
66. Technical Evaluation*
68. Institutional Evaluation*
69. The Cooperative Agreement as a Mechanism for Technology Utilization*
86. Experiment in Contractor Selection*
87. Management of Federal Civilian Research and Development Program*
112. R&D Projects (evaluation)*
115. Exploratory Analysis*
128. Campus-Community Integrated Utility System*

SMALL BUSINESS

9. Imperfections in Capital Markets
28. Assisting Small Firms Required by Regulation to Undergo Technological Change
32. Connecticut Product Development Corporation
46. Competency Evaluation of Small R&D Firms
77. Symposium in Assistance to Small Technology-Based Firms
78. Data Collection, Summarization, and Interpretation for ETIP Project with Connecticut Product Development Corporation
79. Survey of Five-Year Results of Innovation Loan Program
89. The Connecticut Experiment
10. Analysis of Reasons for Nonacquisition of Independent Inventions by Corporations and Patent Broker/Developers*
20. Creation of National Product Marketing Service*
27. Development of Procedures for Evaluating Technology-Based Firms for SBA Funding*
113. Test Loan Evaluation Procedure*
114. Test Small Business Regulatory Compliance Procedures*

ECONOMIC ASSISTANCE

17. Federal Contingency Planning for Anticipated Technological Crisis

 93.   Federal Financial Assistance and Technological Change
132.   Refinement and Dissemination of Policy Issues for Contingency
       Planning and Contingency Planning for Anticipated Crises in Com-
       modity Supplies
135.   Energy Volume Expansion
136.   Small Business (design of analysis)
108.   Monitoring Assistance*

APPENDIX D

PROJECT PARTNERS

Project	Lead Agency	Cooperating Agency(-ies)
1	FSS	EPA, CPSC, OSHA, OPEI
2	FSS	EPA, DoD, AHAM
3	FSS	DoD, AHAM
4	FSS	DoD, AHAM, GAMA
5	FSS	DoD, AHAM, GAMA
7	ETIP	CPSC, NBS
8	ETIP	—
9	ETIP	SBA
11	ETIP	
13	NSF	
17	ETIP	Treasury Department, CEA
19	ETIP	
28	SBA	
29	ETIP	FSS, Treasury Department, HEW
31	FRA	DoT, ICC
32	ETIP	
36	FSS	NBS
38	ETIP	DoD
40	ETIP	FSS
41	ETIP	FSS
42	FSS	
44	ETIP	ICC, FCC, FPC
45	ETIP	EPA, OSHA
46	SBA	
47	AEC	NBS, NRC
48	EPA	
59	FSS	

60	ETIP	FSS, CSG
63	FSS	
64	FSS	
67	HEW	NBS
70	FSS	
72	ETIP	
74	FSS	
75	ETIP	FSS, NBS
76	FPC	
77	ETIP	SBA
78	ETIP	
79	ETIP	SBA
80	VA	
85	OSHA	
88	FDA	NBS
89	ETIP	
93	ETIP	NSF, DoT, OMB, DoC, JEC
94	ETIP	NAS
95	ETIP	
96	ETIP	HEW
97	ETIP	
116	ETIP	FSS
118	FSS	
119	ETIP	FSS
120	ETIP	FSS, NASPO, NIGP, VA
121	ETIP	FSS, NASPO, NIGP, VA
123	ETIP	FSS
124	ETIP	
125	ETIP	CPSC, NBS
126	ETIP	
127	ABA	NAE
129	FSS	NBS
130	ETIP	
131	FSS	
132	ETIP	DoC, DoI, DoD, GSA, NSF
134	ETIP	
135	ETIP	ERDA, FEA
136	ETIP	
137	ETIP	FSS

REFERENCES

Allen, L. A. (1958) Management and Organization. New York: McGraw-Hill.
Arensberg, Conrad (1941) "Toward a 'control' system for industrial relations." Applied Anthropology 1:54-57.
——— (1978) "Theoretical contributions of industrial and development studies," in E. M. Eddy and W. L. Partridge (eds.) Applied Anthropology in America. New York: Columbia University Press.
Blau, Peter M. (1954) The Dynamics of Bureaucracy: A Study of Interpersonal Relations in Two Government Agencies. Chicago: University of Chicago Press.
——— and W. Richard Schoenherr (1971) The Structure of Organizations. New York: Basic Books.
Braverman, Harry (1975) Labor and Monopoly Capital: The Degradation of Work in the Twentieth Century. New York: Monthly Review Press.
Brech, E.F.L. (1957) Organization. New York: Longman.
Brim, John and David Spain (1974) Research Design in Anthropology. New York: Holt, Rinehart & Winston.
Britan, Gerald M. (1977) "Public policy and innovation: a report to the ETIP Evaluation Panel." National Academy of Sciences, Washington, D.C.
——— (1978a) "The place of anthropology in program evaluation." Anthropological Quarterly 51: 119-128.
——— (1978b) "Experimental and contextual models of program evaluation." Evaluation and Program Planning 1: 229-234.
——— (1979a) "Some problems of fieldwork in the federal bureaucracy." Anthropoligical Quarterly 52: 211-220.
——— (1979b) "Evaluating a federal experiment in bureaucratic reform." Human Organization 38: 319-324.
——— and Michael Chibnik [eds.] (1977) Case Studies in Public Policy Experimentation: A Report to the ETIP Evaluation Panel. Washington, DC: National Academy of Sciences.
——— (1980) "Bureaucracy and innovation: an American case," in G. M. Britan and R. Cohen (eds.) Hierarchy and Society. Philadelphia: ISHI.
Britan, Gerald M. and Ronald Cohen (1980a) "Towards an anthropology of formal organizations," in G. M. Britan and R. Cohen (eds.) Hierarchy and Society. Philadelphia: ISHI.
——— (1980b) Hierarchy and Society: Anthropological Perspectives on Bureaucracy. Philadelphi: ISHI.
Browner, Carole and Michael Chibnik (1979) "Anthropoligical research for a computer manufacturing company." Central Issues in Anthropology 1: 63-76.

Buraway, Michael (1975) "The hegemonic organization of industrial work." Presented at the annual meeting of the American Sociological Society.
Chapple, Eliot D. (1941) "Organization problems in industry." Applied Anthropology 1: 2-9.
Cicourel, S. (1974) "General semantics and the structure of social interaction," in Cognitive Sociology. New York: Free Press.
Cohen, Ronald (1977) "A study of R&D funding," in G. M. Britan and M. Chibnik (eds.) Case Studies in Public Policy Experimentation. Washington, DC: National Academy of Sciences.
Connolly, Terry (1977) "Information processing and decision-making in organizations," in B. M. Staw and G. R. Solncik (eds.) New Directions in Organization Behavior. Chicago: St. Clair Press.
Davis, Allison W., Burleigh B. Gardner, and Mary R. Gardner (1941) Deep South: A Social-Anthropological Study of Caste and Class. Chicago: University of Chicago Press.
Downs, George W., Jr., and Lawrence Mohr (1976) "Conceptual issues in the study of innovation." Administrative Science Quarterly 21: 700-714.
Eads, George (1974) "U.S. government support for civilian technology: economic theory versus political practice." Research Policy 3, 1.
――― and Richard R. Nelson (1971) Governmental support of advanced civilian technology: power reactors and the supersonic transport. Public Policy 14, 1: 405-427.
Experimental Technology Incentives Program [ETIP] (1972) ETIP. Gaithersburg, MD: National Bureau of Standards.
――― (1973) ETIP. Gaithersburg, MD: National Bureau of Standards.
――― (1974) Program Plan 1974. Gaithersburg, MD: National Bureau of Standards.
――― (1975) Progress Report. Gaithersburg, MD: National Bureau of Standards.
――― (1976) Briefing Book. Gaithersburg, MD: National Bureau of Standards.
――― (1977) Area Plan for Fiscal 1977. Gaithersburg, MD: National Bureau of Standards.
Foster, George (1969) Applied Anthropology. Boston: Little, Brown.
Gamst, Frederick C. (1977) Industrial Ethnology. Anthropological Quarterly 50.
Gardner, Burleigh B. (1945) Human Relations in Industry. Homewood, IL: Irwin.
Gilpen, Robert (1975) Technology, Economic Growth, and International Competitiveness. Washington, DC: Government Printing Office.
Goldman, Daniel R. (1973) "Managerial mobility motivations and central life interests." American Sociological Review 38: 119-126.
Gouldner, Alvin W. (1954) "Patterns of industrial bureaucracy." New York: Free Press.
Gulick, L. and L. Urwick (1937) Papers on the Science of Administration. New York: Institute of Public Administration.
Hall, Richard H., J. Eugene Hass, and Norman J. Johnson (1967) "Organizational size, complexity, and formalization." American Sociological Review 32: 904-912.
Hill, Larry B. (1976) The Model Ombudsman. Princeton: Princeton University Press.
Hufbauer, G. C. (1966) Synthetic Materials and the Theory of International Trade. London: Duckworth.
Kanter, Rosabeth (1977) Men and Women of the Corporation. New York: Basic Books.

Karpic, Lucien (1972) "Le capitalisme technologique." Sociologie du Travail 14, 1: 2-34.

Keesing, D. B. (1967) "The impact of research and development on United States trade." Journal of Political Economy 75, 1: 38-48.

Kottenstette, J. P. and J. J. Rusnak (1973) "Transfer and diffusion—two ways to transmit technology." Research Management 4: 24-27.

Lawler, Edward E. (1973) Motivation in Organization. Belmont, CA: Wadsworth.

McNeil, Ken (1971) The Regeneration of Social Organization. American Sociological Review 36: 624-637.

Mansfield, E. (1968) The Economics of Technological Change. New York: Norton.

Mayo, Elton (1940) The Human Problems of an Industrial Civilization. New York: Viking.

Moonay, J. D. and A. C. Reiley (1931) Onward Industry. New York: Harper & Row.

Naroll, Raoul and Ronald Cohen [eds.] (1970) A Handbook of Method in Cultural Anthropology. New York: Columbia University Press.

National Bureau of Standards [NBS] (1972) CTAB Memo. Gaithersburg, MD: Author.

Nelson, Richard (1971) "World leadership, the 'technology gap,' and national policy." Minerva 9, 1: 386-399.

———, Merton Peck, and Edward Kalachek (1967) Technology, Economic Growth and Public Policy. Washington, DC: Brookings.

Nixon, Richard (1972) President's Annual Budget Message. Washington, DC: Government Printing Office.

Pelto, Pertti S. (1978) Anthropoligical Research: The Structure of Inquiry. New York: Harper & Row.

Perrow, Charles (1972) Complex Organizations: A Critical Essay. Glenview, IL: Scott, Foresman.

Pettigrew, Andrew M. (1973) The Politics of Organizational Decision-Making. London: Tavistock.

Pugh, D. S., D. J. Hickson, C. R. Hinings, K. M. MacDonald, C. Turner, and T. Lupton (1963) "A conceptual scheme for organizational analysis." Administrative Science Quarterly 8: 289-315.

Pugh, D. S., D. J. Hickson, C. R. Hinings, and C. Turner (1968) "Dimensions of organization structure." Administrative Science Quarterly 13: 65-105.

Radnor, Michael et al. [eds.] (1978) "The diffusion of innovation: an assessment." Center for the Interdisciplinary Study of Science and Technology, Northwestern University.

Richardson, Frederick L. W. (1941) "Community resettlement in a depressed coal region." Applied Anthropology 1: 24-53.

——— (1961) Talk, Work, and Action. Monograph No. 3. Ithaca, NY: Society for Applied Anthropology.

Riecken, H. W., R. F. Boruch, D. T. Campbell, N. Caplan, T. K. Glennan, J. Pratt, A. Rees, and W. Williams (1974) Social Experimentation. New York: Academic.

Roethlisberger, F. J. and W. J. Dickson (1939) Management and the Worker. Cambridge, MA: Harvard University Press.

Rule, James (1979) Insight and Social Betterment. New York: Oxford University Press.

Schwartzman, Helen B. (1980) "The bureaucratic context of a community health center: the view from up," in G. M. Britan and R. Cohen (eds.) Hierarchy and Society. Philadelphia: Institute for the Study of Human Issues.
———, A. Kneifel, and M. Krouse (1978) "Culture conflict in a community mental health center." Journal of Social Issues 34: 93-110.
Scott, William G. (1961) "Organization theory: an overview and an appraisal." Journal of the Academy of Management 4: 7-26.
Selznick, P. (1949) TVA and the Grass Roots. Berkeley: University of California Press.
Simon, Herbert (1974) Administrative Behavior. New York: Free Press.
Spradley, James (1979) The Ethnographic Interview. New York: Holt, Rinehart & Winston.
Tassey, Gregory (1975) "Federal subsidies and capital formation: some economic policy elements." (unpublished)
Taylor, R. W. (1911) Principles of Scientific Management. New York: Harper & Row.
Thompson, Victor A. (1961) Modern Organizations. New York: Knopf.
Tourane, Alain (1971) Post-Industrial Society. New York: Random House.
Vernon, Raymond (1966) International Investment and International Trade in the Product Cycle. Quarterly Journal of Economics (May): 190-207.
Vivelo, Frank (1980) "Anthropology, applied research, and non-academic careers." (unpublished)
Warner, W. L. and J. Low (1947) The Social System of the Modern Factory. New Haven, CT: Yale University Press.
Weber, Max (1947) The Theory of Social and Economic Organization. New York: Free Press.
Weidenbaum, Murray (1965) "Government encouragement of private sector research and development." Studies in Comparative International Development 1, 9.
Whyte, William Foote (1955) Money and Motivation. New York: Harper & Row.
——— (1975) Organizing for Agricultural Development. New Brunswick, NJ: Transaction.
——— (1978) "Organizational behavior research—where do we go from here?" in E. M. Eddy and W. L. Partridge (eds.) Applied Anthropology in America. New York: Columbia University Press.
Williams, Thomas Rhys (1967) Field Methods in the Study of Culture. New York: Holt, Rinehart & Winston.
Zald, Mayer N. (1970) Organizational Change. Chicago: University of Chicago Press.

ABOUT THE AUTHOR

Gerald M. Britan is Assistant Professor of Anthropology and Urban Affairs at Northwestern University, and Co-Director of Northwestern University's Program in Ethnography and Public Policy. During 1980-1981 he has been on leave from Northwestern to serve as a Senior Policy Analyst for the U.S. Department of Agriculture. He has conducted major research projects on social and economic change in Newfoundland and on bureaucratic reform in Washington, D.C., as well as numerous short-term evaluations of education and social action programs throughout the country. He has served as a consultant to the National Academy of Sciences, the Agency for International Development, the American Bar Association, and a number of local programs and private corporations. He has written numerous articles, reports, and professional papers on social change, human ecology, bureaucracy, organizational behavior, evaluation research, and applied anthropology, and is the author of *The Schooner Fishermen: Behavior and Change in a Newfoundland Community* (Holt, Rinehart & Winston, forthcoming) and coeditor of *Hierarchy and Society: Anthropological Perspectives on Bureaucracy* (Institute for the Study of Human Issues, 1980).